The Way to
Paradise

Allah's Word in the Holy Bible
about Life after Death for Muslims

Renod Bejjani

The Way to Paradise
©2019 by Renod Bejjani

All rights reserved. No part of this publication may be reproduced in any form or by any electronic or mechanical means, including information storage and retrieval systems, without permission in writing by the publisher, except by a reviewer who may quote brief passages in a review. For information regarding permission, contact the publisher at info@WordOfAllah.org.

> This book is available at special discounts when purchased in quantity for use as premiums, promotions, fundraisers, or for educational use. For inquiries and details, contact the publisher at info@WordOfAllah.org.

Published by iHOPE Ministries

Editing and Interior Design by My Writers' Connection

Scripture quotations taken from The Holy Bible, New International Version® NIV®, ©1973 1978 1984 2011 by Biblica, Inc.™ Used by permission. All rights reserved worldwide.

Library of Congress Control Number: 2019916619
Paperback ISBN: 978-1-951-616-00-7
Ebook ISBN: 978-1-951616-01-4

First Printing: December 2019

Contents

As-Salaam Alaikum!..v
Chapter One: Only One Way to Paradise 1
Chapter Two: Allah's Word.. 11
Chapter Three: Allah's Story and Revelations about Himself 23
Chapter Four: Allah's Creation... 37
Chapter Five: Sin and Shame... 55
Chapter Six: Ibrahim and Sacrifice 71
Chapter Seven: Musa, Israel, and Sacrifice 87
Chapter Eight: Allah's Requirement.................................. 101
Chapter Nine: Allah's Law.. 119
Chapter Ten: Allah's Promised Servant and Savior 139
Chapter Eleven: Jesus 155
Chapter Twelve: Jesus (Part Two)..................................... 173
Chapter Thirteen: Allah 199
Chapter Fourteen: The Why.. 219
Chapter Fifteen: The End Times.. 247
Chapter Sixteen: Allah's Expectations of YOU 275
About the Author 285

As-Salaam Alaikum!

I pray, *insha'Allah* (God willing in English), I will meet you in person someday soon. It would bless me to know you and be known by you, while enjoying a meal and/or a refreshing beverage together. If circumstances do not give us the opportunity to meet in person, then I pray, insha'Allah, we will meet in Paradise where you and I can enjoy eternal life with Allah.

Meanwhile, I would like to ask you, "Why are you reading this book?"

Whatever your reason, I am humbled, honored, and privileged to study with you the most important parts of what Allah (God in English, *Alahi* in Aramaic) reveals in the Holy Bible. We will focus on some of what Allah reveals about Himself and His holy plan to restore humanity—you and me—to eternal Paradise with Him.

It is in the Holy Bible that Allah reveals that there is and can be only One Way for us to have eternal life in Paradise. Not two or more ways, only One! The good news is that Allah reveals this One Way clearly in the Holy Bible, and He guarantees entrance to Paradise to every person who follows this Way!

For me, that journey of discovering Allah's Way to Paradise began around twenty-five years ago (I will share more with you about that journey throughout this book). I read what Allah said in Jeremiah 31:3 (New International Version):

> *"... I have loved you with an everlasting love; I have drawn you with unfailing kindness."*

I pray that you realize, as I did back then, that this verse (and many others like it throughout the Holy Bible) applies to you. Allah loves you with an everlasting love! Through this book, Allah is drawing "you with unfailing kindness." I pray you will respond to Allah as I did. My sincere hope is that you will read this book all the way through and discover Allah's Word and great love for you.

You may find, as I did initially, that understanding Allah's love letter to you, the Holy Bible, can be challenging at times. But I also discovered many verses in the Holy Bible where Allah promises understanding for those who seek Him wholeheartedly. For example:

JEREMIAH 29:13 (NIV)

> *"You will seek me and find me when you seek me with all your heart."*

JAMES 1:5 (NIV)

> *"If any of you lacks wisdom, you should ask God (Allah), who gives generously to all without finding fault, and it will be given to you."*

So join me, and let us seek Allah wholeheartedly together. Ask Allah to give you wisdom and understanding. Allah will do with you as He promised in the above verses, just as He did and does with me even today. Ask Allah to open your spiritual eyes and heart to what He wants you to see and understand from His love letter to you. Allah will!

Having a close, loving relationship with anyone takes time and effort. But the relationship is always worth it! The same is true of your relationship with Allah. He is inviting you to know Him and enjoy a close, loving relationship with Him. In this book, we will study together the One and only Way Allah says this is possible. I encourage you to read all the way through so you will discover how Allah makes this relationship with Him possible, in your daily life now, and with you for eternity in Paradise.

In my own journey of getting to know Allah, I discovered that when we love Him and follow His Way, He gives us a heavenly life right now on earth. This doesn't mean that our lives suddenly become perfect or easy, but that we experience a heavenly life in the mind, heart, and soul. My inner life used to be more like hell on earth. In the Holy Bible (Galatians 5), Allah describes what it was like for me to feel alone and lost in self-centered desires and habits such as "sexual immorality, impurity and debauchery, idolatry . . . hatred, discord, jealousy, fits of rage, selfish ambition, dissensions, factions, and envy."

But through the process of discovering Allah's Word in the Holy Bible about His One and only Way to Paradise, Allah has filled me with His Holy Spirit. His Holy Spirit in turn filled me with what Allah promises in the Holy Bible, "love, joy, peace, forbearance, kindness, goodness, faithfulness, gentleness, and self-control" (Galatians 5:23). Allah wants to do the same with you!

Allah is inviting you right now:

REVELATION 3:20 (NIV)

"Here I am! I stand at the door and knock. If anyone hears my voice and opens the door, I will come in and eat with that person, and they with me."

Chapter One

Only One Way to Paradise

Allah began inspiring the writing of the Holy Bible around 3,500 years ago and completed it nearly 1,925 years ago. Allah revealed His Word over a period of 1,575 years, through different prophets, most of whom never met or knew each other, on three continents (Africa, Asia, and Europe). Together, these inspired revelations comprise the Holy Bible, which gives us a complete story that fits together perfectly. Allah revealed it all this way so that we can be confident in His only Way to Paradise.

It is in the Holy Bible that Allah reveals that there is and can be only One Way for us to have eternal life in Paradise. Not two or more ways, only One! The good news is that Allah reveals this One Way clearly, and He guarantees entrance to Paradise to every person who follows this Way!

This One Way that Allah reveals in the Holy Bible is so important to our eternal destination—yours and mine—that He used more than forty prophets and messengers as witnesses to make sure we got the message. He *wants* you and I to be saved from hell on Judgment Day.

Take a look at one of Allah's revelations in the Holy Bible that give us a glimpse into what Paradise will be like.

REVELATION 21:3-4 (NIV)

... Look! God's (Allah's) dwelling place is now among the people, and he will dwell with them. They will be his people, and God (Allah) himself will be with them and be their God. He will wipe every tear from their eyes. There will be no more death or mourning or crying or pain, for the old order of things has passed away.

Allah's Book of Life

The Book of Life is a record of all the people who will be allowed to enter Paradise. In the Holy Bible, Allah reveals that only the people who have followed His One and only Way have their names written in the Book of Life. It is only those people who will be welcomed into eternal Paradise. Here are two of Allah's revelations about what Judgment Day will look like for those whose names are not written in the Book of Life:

REVELATION 20:15 (NIV)

"Anyone whose name was not found written in the book of life was thrown into the lake of fire."

REVELATION 21:27 (NIV)

"Nothing impure will ever enter it (Paradise) ... but only those whose names are written in the ... book of life."

Allah Loves You!

Allah clearly revealed the way to Paradise and His desire for an eternal relationship with you in the Scriptures because He loves you! The Holy Bible describes Allah's love this way in 1 John 4:7-8:

> Dear friends, let us love one another, for love comes from God (Allah). Everyone who loves has been born of God (Allah) and knows God (Allah). Whoever does not love does not know God (Allah), because God (Allah) is love.

Allah *is* love! It is because of His great love for you that He has made a way for you to live with Him eternally in Paradise. He promises that your name will be written in the Book of Life when you follow His Way to eternal Paradise.

It is because of Allah's great love that I love you, even though we have never met. It is not natural for a weak human being like me to love a person he has never met, but because Allah loves you, the Holy Spirit of Allah put His love for you in my heart. It is Allah's love for you that fills me, so I love you.

But love for others *isn't* what I used to feel toward others—especially Muslims. Let me explain. For many years, I didn't feel love toward Muslims. In truth, I hated Muslims. You see, I was born and raised in the Middle East and North Africa as a Christian among Muslims. Most Muslims were our friends, but I endured intense persecution for my Christian faith from a few extremists. I suffered kidnappings, torture, and the dangers of war before fleeing to the United States at age thirteen. Those horrible and painful experiences left me scarred by anger and hate toward Muslims—and even toward Allah.

For a time, I doubted Allah's existence. In my hurt and anger, I mistakenly thought that if Allah exists, He surely would not allow such terrible things to happen to an innocent child like me. So I stopped believing in the existence of Allah. But as I sought to disprove the existence of any god, through much research and study, I eventually came to believe that there is a Creator.

Then I wanted to determine which god is the true one. So I studied the various major religions of the world, including Islam and Christianity. I read the Quran and the Holy Bible. All the while, Allah refused to give up on me. He kept revealing Himself to me through the things I read in the Holy Bible, through my family, and even through the worst of circumstances. Eventually, I understood that Allah *did* love me. From all that I had studied and learned, I knew that I needed to accept Jesus Christ as my Savior. When I did, Jesus removed the anger and hate from my bitter heart and replaced it with His healing, peace, and love for Muslims. Because of what Jesus has done for me, I can honestly say I love Muslims.

Allah compels me to share His love with them—with *you*. That's why I wrote this book. I want you to know about Allah's love for you and for His great desire for you to know Him. I want you to know that wherever you are He loves you.

Throughout my life, I have observed that many other Christians are how I used to be: angry with and/or afraid of Muslims. In 2011, my wife, Karen, and I founded a teaching ministry called iHOPE Ministries to help other Christians experience the same transformation from fear to love that Jesus had worked in our lives. Since then, Allah has blessed us with thousands of Christian students worldwide who now also love Muslims and share the love of Allah with them.

Allah has also blessed us with thousands of Muslims whom we have met and had the opportunity to love through the years.

Insha'Allah we will meet you in person someday. Meanwhile, I am grateful to take this journey with you to discover what Allah reveals in the Holy Bible so together you and I can enjoy eternal life with Him.

How to Use This Book to Discover Allah's Revelations in the Holy Bible

Pray. Before you begin each new session, pray that the Holy Spirit (*Al-Ruwh Al Quds* in Arabic) of Allah will fill you to reveal, guide, and teach you the truth as we study Allah's revelations together.

1. **Read the Holy Scripture text provided.** The best way to get to know Allah is to read His inspired Word. I've included passages of the Holy Bible in this book for easy reference. Allah has preserved His Word for us to read today. While there are a number of translations, they all have the same message. In this book, the scriptures you'll read in English are from the New International Version (NIV). This modern translation was done by Holy Bible scholars from original manuscripts, which are Allah-breathed originally in the Hebrew, Aramaic, and Greek languages.

    If you prefer to read these passages in another language or translation, please feel free to do so. If possible, download a free Holy Bible app on your computer or smart device (cell phone, tablet, etc.). One that some of our Muslim friends enjoy is **bible.is**. This free app is available as online text and audio in hundreds of languages. If your first language is not English, you may get even more out of the passages by using the bible.is app to read them in the language with which you are most comfortable. Whatever translation you choose, I recommend one that is easy for you to understand.

2. **Ask questions.** I provide a set of questions after each Holy Scripture throughout the study as a guide to help maximize your understanding of what Allah reveals. You may have other questions of your own. Pray that the Holy Spirit of Allah will answer your questions.

3. **Seek answers in the Holy Bible.** Allah has already revealed answers to all questions that have eternal impact in the pages of

the Holy Bible. If you are studying in a printed Holy Bible, you may see comments at the bottom of the page that are written by groups of Christian Holy Bible scholars. Often, these comments point you to other related Holy Scriptures and answers that Allah revealed throughout the Holy Bible.

If you are doing this study with a Christian friend, try not to rely on him or her to reveal answers to you. We are all imperfect human beings, and we do not have all the right answers. Your Christian friend may, however, be able to help you find answers for yourself in the Holy Bible. Whenever possible, it is best to seek answers from the Holy Spirit of Allah and what He reveals in the Holy Bible.

If you do not find answers through these processes or you do not know nor have access to a Christian near you, then please contact us via email (answers@WordofAllah.org). Someone from our team will seek to answer your questions as soon as possible. If you would like, we can also try to connect you with a Christian near you.

4. **Use an app or other study tool.** Many printed copies of the Holy Bible include a concordance in the back. The concordance is prepared by groups of Christian Holy Bible scholars. It lists words and names that readers most frequently look up when studying a Holy Bible. If the word or name you look up is in the concordance, you will see that it points to sections, chapters, and verses where that term is used elsewhere in the Holy Bible.

If you are studying the Holy Bible through an app, you can search for a word, name, or phrase (for example, *marriage, love, faith, hope*, etc.). That process may guide you to verses throughout the Holy Bible that may answer your questions.

5. **Obey what Allah teaches you through these Holy Scriptures.** Allah blesses faithful obedience and through that process reveals more truth.

6. **Pray after each session.** If you are doing this study with a Christian friend, then after each session, ask that person to pray to Allah for you in the name of Jesus.

> ### How to Find Holy Scriptures in the Holy Bible
>
> The Holy Bible combines sixty-six little Holy Books to form one complete Holy Book. Each little Holy Book has a name. In either a printed or digital copy of the Holy Bible, you will usually see a table of contents at the beginning that will refer you to the page number where each little Holy Book begins. Each little book is divided into chapters and verses.
>
> In each section of our study together, I will ask you to find and read a specific chapter and verse number within one of these little Holy Books; for example, when I ask you to read Deuteronomy 4:29, that means find the little Holy Book Deuteronomy in the table of contents of the Holy Bible you have, turn to chapter 4, and read verse 29.
>
> I will include the text of the verse or verses from the Holy Bible in this book. But it is more helpful to you to find the verses in the Holy Bible you are using. It is there you will read what Allah breathed out to a specific prophet or messenger in order to reveal it to you today. By looking up the Scriptures yourself, you can read the entire Holy Scripture for proper context of what Allah is revealing. If I insert anything into the text for clarification, you will see the insertion in parentheses ( ).

Why Do Christians Pray "in the name of Jesus"?

Allah reveals in the Holy Bible that Jesus "lives to intercede for them" (meaning you and me) with Allah. Jesus is our advocate and through Him we can " . . . then approach God's (Allah's) throne of grace with confidence so that we may receive mercy and find grace to help us in our time of need" (Hebrews 4:16).

- So ask a Christian friend to pray to Allah with you in the name of Jesus. If you do not know or have access to a Christian near you, then please contact us with your specific prayer request (pray@WordofAllah.org).

When you pray, be specific with any need or issue that Allah can do for you today, even if it is miraculous. Allah does not always perform physical miracles when we pray, but He wants us to talk to Him and trust Him with our fears, hurts, and needs. He has already accomplished the greatest miracle of all time, which is providing The Way for you and me to have eternal life with Him in Paradise. In this book, we will study how you can have this greatest miracle from Allah. It is already yours if you choose it.

Meanwhile, Allah does desire the best for His children. Allah is all knowing; He knows if a physical miracle would bring us more harm than good. He may choose not to answer your prayers in the way you may hope or anticipate. But He always listens and always does what He knows will draw us closer to Him. With that in mind, I personally witnessed, experienced, and know of eleven physical miracles Allah has done out of the hundreds of Muslims I have prayed with in the name of Jesus. Here is one.

A Miraculous Physical Healing

"Mohsen," a Muslim refugee, fled war in his country and moved to a new one where I met him. Although he had been a construction worker since he was a teenager, it was difficult for him to get a job in construction in the country where he had moved. Financially, Mohsen was very poor. He needed to work to support his wife and four young children, so he was thankful when he finally got a job.

One day on his way home after work, Mohsen was involved in a severe accident in which his arms were crushed. Mohsen was not well educated; his only skill was as a construction worker. With his arms crushed, he could no longer do manual labor. Without any source of income, Mohsen and his young family became financially destitute.

"Paul," a Christian neighbor who knew of the accident and the situation, offered to pray with Mohsen in the name of Jesus. Mohsen did not understand the reference about the name of Jesus, or why that seemed important, but he felt desperate, so he accepted Paul's offer. Paul prayed to Allah, asking for miraculous physical healing for Mohsen. At the end of the prayer, Paul said, "In the name of Jesus, amen."

Instantly, Mohsen's crushed arms were healed, the bones and muscles strengthened, and Mohsen could suddenly use his arms again. After a period of praising Allah and celebration, Mohsen asked Paul about why he prayed in the name of Jesus. Paul shared with Mohsen that Allah teaches about praying in the name of Jesus in the Holy Bible. Mohsen started discovering the Holy Bible with Paul. They began the journey by looking at a miracle recorded in Acts chapter 3, verse 6: " . . . In the name of Jesus Christ (Al-Masih in Arabic) of Nazareth, walk."

Here's part of the story from Acts 3:1–8:

One day Peter and John were going up to the temple at the time of prayer—at three in the afternoon. Now a man who was lame from birth was being carried to the temple gate called Beautiful, where he was put every day to beg from those going into the temple courts. When he saw Peter and John about to enter, he asked them for money. Peter looked straight at him, as did John. Then Peter said, "Look at us!" So the man gave them his attention, expecting to get something from them.

Then Peter said, "Silver or gold I do not have, but what I do have I give you. In the name of Jesus Christ (Al-Masih) of Nazareth, walk." Taking him by the right hand, he helped him up, and instantly the man's feet and ankles became strong. He jumped to his feet and began to walk. Then he went with them into the temple courts, walking and jumping, and praising God (Allah).

The Greatest Miracle

Physical miracles are indeed awesome. You will read about many more that Jesus Christ performed in the Holy Bible. But as I mentioned earlier, Allah does not always respond to our prayers the way we ask Him to. He may not choose to bring you or a loved one physical healing, but He always offers miraculous spiritual healing. That is Allah's greatest miracle, and it is what He desires for you. His gift of eternal life in Paradise is a miracle—one that He has already accomplished. I am excited to begin this journey with you so you can discover how you can have this greatest miracle from Allah.

Chapter Two

Allah's Word

Let us begin with a prayer:

We pray that the Holy Spirit of Allah will fill our hearts and minds to reveal, guide, and teach us the truth as we discover Allah's revelations in the Holy Bible. In Jesus's name, amen!

Allah reveals in the Holy Bible that there is only One Way you and I can be saved from hell and enter into eternal life in Paradise. In my own journey to discover the truth about Allah, I believed it was vital to know if the words in the Holy Bible are truly Allah's words. In this chapter, we will study this foundational issue: Is the Holy Bible truly Allah's Word?

Seek Allah

To answer that important question, Allah states that first we must seek Allah sincerely and wholeheartedly. Please turn to and read about that in the following Holy Scriptures:

DEUTERONOMY 4:29

"But if from there you seek the Lord your God, you will find him if you seek him with all your heart and with all your soul."

JEREMIAH 29:13

"You will seek me and find me when you seek me with all your heart."

Notes

- Deuteronomy (*Altathnia* in Arabic) was Allah-breathed through nabi Musa (the prophet Moses in English) around 3,425 years ago.
- Jeremiah (*Irmiya* in Arabic) was Allah-breathed around 2,575 years ago.

Please pause here and ponder what you've read.

- Explain the passages in your own words as if you were sharing it with someone else.
- Explain how the passages make you think or feel and why.
- What do the passages tell you about Allah?
- What do the passages tell you about you and your relationship with Allah?
- What action do you think Allah wants from you according to these passages?
- Based on what you have learned about Allah, create an "I will . . ." statement to obey what He has revealed according to this passage. For example, my statement in connection with the above verses would be, "I will schedule thirty minutes every day to wholeheartedly seek a close relationship with Allah daily through studying His Word in the Holy Bible."

Allah's Word Is Forever

ISAIAH 40:8

"The grass withers and the flowers fall, but the Word of our God endures forever."

MARK 13:31

"Heaven and earth will pass away, but my words will never pass away."

Notes

- Isaiah (Asheia in Arabic) was Allah-breathed through the prophet around 2,750 years ago.
- Mark (Markus in Arabic) was Allah-breathed around 2,000 years ago.

Allah's Word Is Flawless

PSALM 18:30

"As for God (Allah), His way is perfect. The Lord's Word is flawless; He shields all who take refuge in Him."

PROVERBS 30:5

"Every word of God (Allah) is flawless; He is a shield to those who take refuge in Him."

Notes

- Psalms is known as Zabur by Muslims and was translated as Almazamir in Arabic. Allah breathed most of the words in Psalms around 3,000 years ago.

- Proverbs (Alamthal in Arabic) was Allah-breathed around 2,900 years ago.

The Holy Bible Is Allah's Word

2 TIMOTHY 3:16

"All Scripture is God-breathed (Allah-breathed) and is useful for teaching, rebuking, correcting and training in righteousness."

2 PETER 1:20–21

"Above all, you must understand that no prophecy of Scripture came about by the prophet's own interpretation of things. For prophecy never had its origin in the human will, but prophets, though human, spoke from God (Allah) as they were carried along by the Holy Spirit."

Notes

- 2 Timothy was Allah-breathed around 1,950 years ago.
- 2 Peter was Allah-breathed around 1,955 years ago.

Please pause here and think about these verses.

- Explain the passages in your own words as if you were sharing it with someone else.
- Explain how the passages make you think or feel and why.
- What do the passages tell you about Allah?
- What do the passages tell you about you and your relationship with Allah?
- What action do you think Allah wants from you according to these passages?

- As a result, create an "I will . . ." statement to obey Allah according to these passages.

Chapter Conclusion

As I shared in the introduction to this book, during my journey to seek the truth regarding Allah, I studied the writings of several major religions, including the Quran and the Holy Bible. Along the way, I concluded that the truth had to be contained within Islam, Christianity, or both. I saw many similarities between these two faiths; for example, both religions share a belief in the eternal afterlife, either in Paradise or in hell. But I also saw some critical differences between Islam and Christianity.

Islam and Christianity Are Opposites in This . . .

Regarding the way to heaven (Paradise), the two religions are exactly the opposite. If I were to follow the Islamic way, the revelation of Allah in the Holy Bible states that I would be rejecting the only Way to eternal Paradise. With my eternal destination in mind, I knew I had to choose one as the truth. So I prayed to Allah to reveal the truth as I studied deeper.

In studying Islam deeper, I understood that my Muslim friends believe that Allah revealed his word through the archangel Jibril (Gabriel in English) to the Prophet Muhammad over a period of about twenty-three years while he was alone. Later, after the Prophet Muhammad recited the revelation, some of his followers wrote down the words to form the Holy Quran.

In contrast, the Holy Bible is Allah-breathed through forty different prophets and messengers, most of whom did not personally know each other. Allah did so for nearly 1,575 years, on three different continents. Even though the writings in the Holy Bible span centuries, together these scriptures form a complete story that fits together perfectly. In the Holy Bible, Allah repeatedly declares that His Word is perfect, flawless, that it endures forever, and will never pass away. Allah also reveals in the Holy Bible that there is only One Way to eternal life in Paradise and that He guarantees entrance to Paradise to the person who follows that One Way.

I had to consider the differences between a revelation claimed by one human for twenty-three years, and the combined revelations claimed by forty different humans over 1,575 years, on three continents. As I prayed wholeheartedly for Allah's Holy Spirit to reveal the truth to me, I finally concluded that Allah, as He claimed repeatedly, protected His Word in the Holy Bible, and that no one can change the Word of Allah. I believed in His One Way to Paradise, and I accepted the gift of eternal salvation that He revealed to me through the Holy Bible.

Will You Pray for Allah to Reveal the Truth to You About His Word and Way?

Let us close this session with prayer.

- What specific requests do you have for Allah now?
- If you have a Christian friend, then ask him or her to pray with you in the name of Jesus.
- If you do not know or have access to a Christian near you, then please contact us with your specific prayer request (pray@WordofAllah.org).

Be specific with any need or issue that Allah can do for you today, even if it is miraculous. It does not mean that Allah will perform a physical miracle for you. The greatest miracle Allah desires for you is eternal life in Paradise, and He has already accomplished that, and it is already yours if you choose it.

Jesus Heals a Man Possessed with a Jinn Spirit

In every chapter I will share with you a story Allah inspires in the Holy Bible about healings He does through Jesus. Insha'Allah you and your loved ones will experience miraculous healing of the best kind as we pray to Allah for you in the name of Jesus. In this chapter, since we studied about Allah's Word, the Holy Spirit of Allah inspired me to share with you a story from the Holy Bible that shows the power of Allah's Word to defeat al Shaytan as well as a modern-day miracle.

LET'S START IN LUKE 4:1–4.

Jesus, full of the Holy Spirit, left the Jordan and was led by the Spirit into the wilderness, where for forty days he was tempted by the devil (al Shaytan in Arabic). He ate nothing during those days, and at the end of them he was hungry. The devil (al Shaytan) said to him, "If you are the Son of God (Allah), tell this stone to become bread."

Jesus answered, "It is written: 'Man shall not live on bread alone.'"

Notes

- Jesus cited Deuteronomy 8:3

PLEASE CONTINUE WITH LUKE 4:5–8.

The devil (al Shaytan) led him up to a high place and showed him in an instant all the kingdoms of the world. And he said to him, "I will give you all their authority and splendor; it has been given to me, and I can give it to anyone I want to. If you worship me, it will all be yours."

Jesus answered, "It is written: 'Worship the Lord your God and serve him only.'"

> **Notes**
>
> - Jesus cited Deuteronomy 6:13 and 1 Samuel 7:3

LUKE 4:9–13

The devil (al Shaytan) led him to Jerusalem and had him stand on the highest point of the temple. "If you are the Son of God (Allah)," he said, "throw yourself down from here. For it is written: 'He will command his angels concerning you to guard you carefully; they will lift you up in their hands, so that you will not strike your foot against a stone.'"

Jesus answered, "It is said: 'Do not put the Lord your God to the test.'"

When the devil (al Shaytan) had finished all this tempting, he left him until an opportune time.

> **Notes**
>
> - Al Shaytan cited Psalm 91:11–12, misusing the Holy Scripture passage. Jesus denounces him by using the Holy Scriptures appropriately in citing Deuteronomy 6:16.

PLEASE MOVE FORWARD TO LUKE 4:31–37.

Then he [Jesus] went down to Capernaum, a town in Galilee, and on the Sabbath he taught the people. They were amazed at this teaching, because his words had authority. In the synagogue there was a man possessed by a demon, an impure spirit. He cried out at the top of his voice, "Go away! What do you want with us, Jesus of Nazareth? Have you come to destroy us? I know who you are—the Holy One of God (Allah)!"

"Be quiet!" Jesus said sternly. "Come out of him!" Then the demon threw the man down before them all and came out without injuring him.

> *All the people were amazed and said to each other, "What words these are! With authority and power he gives orders to impure spirits and they come out!" And the news about him spread throughout the surrounding area.*

Muslim Healed from Demon Possession

A few years ago, an Arabic Muslim family in the Middle East brought their twenty-two-year-old son to Christian partners of iHOPE Ministries who live in their area. They explained that their son, "Hamdi," appeared to have been possessed by demons since he was a teenager. Strange voices spoke from his mouth, saying evil and hateful things. Hamdi often experienced violent fits of rage, seeking to harm himself. It would take the strength of several men to restrain him, fearing he might also harm others.

The Muslim family exhausted all their options, including years of praying twelve times each day at mosques, having imams pray over Hamdi, posting Quran verses, etc. Since nothing up to that point worked, in desperation, they sought iHOPE's Christian partners as they heard of a few reported miracles in response to their prayers to Allah in the name of Jesus.

Seven adult Christians, five males and two females, gathered in a room inside an apartment they used as a "house church." They surrounded Hamdi, all seven praying out loud over him, led by the Christian pastor. They quoted Allah-breathed verses from the Holy Bible, demanding the spirits leave Hamdi, praying to Allah in the name of Jesus.

They prayed this way for more than an hour. The voices coming from Hamdi screamed vile things at the seven Christians praying for him. Repeatedly, in violent fits of rage, he tried to overpower them physically. It took all their strength to restrain him from harming them and himself. Then Hamdi screeched, and suddenly he lay there quietly and peacefully, looking as if he were sleeping.

Minutes later, Hamdi woke up, healed from the spirits that had possessed him for years. Everyone thanked and praised Allah for answering the prayers these Christians offered in the name of Jesus.

Allah Healed Me

As I shared earlier in the introduction to this book, before I accepted Jesus into my heart, it was filled with anger and hate for Muslims. After I accepted Jesus into my heart, Allah filled me with His Holy Spirit. As I began to "walk by the Spirit" (Galatians 5:16), Allah began to transform my heart. The more I walked "by the Spirit," the more I was filled with "the fruit of the Spirit," which is love, joy, peace, patience, kindness, goodness, faithfulness, gentleness, and self-control (Galatians 5:22–23).

I have also experienced physical miracles in my life, but this spiritual transformation is the greatest miracle. I pray that you experience the miracles you need most. Insha'Allah.

Allah's Word Is Light!

PSALM 119:105

Your word is a lamp for my feet, a light on my path.

PSALM 119:9–16

How can a young person stay on the path of purity? By living according to your word.

I seek you with all my heart; do not let me stray from your commands.

I have hidden your word in my heart that I might not sin against you.

Praise be to you, Lord; teach me your decrees.

With my lips I recount all the laws that come from your mouth.

I rejoice in following your statutes as one rejoices in great riches.

I meditate on your precepts and consider your ways.

I delight in your decrees; I will not neglect your word.

Chapter Three

Allah's Story and Revelations about Himself

Let us begin with a prayer:

We pray that the Holy Spirit of Allah will fill us to reveal, guide, and teach us the truth as we discover Allah's story and revelations about Himself in the Holy Bible. In Jesus's name, amen!

The attributes Allah reveals about Himself—His nature, character, and plan for humanity—in the Holy Bible provide a foundation for all we will study together in this book. What we learn about Allah in His Word allows us to discover and better understand His One Way for being saved from hell and allowed to enter eternal Paradise. Let's start this study with an overview of the beginning and the ending of the story to see what Allah reveals in the Holy Bible about His plan for you and me.

Allah begins the revelation of the story in the first book of the Holy Bible, Genesis.

PLEASE TURN TO AND READ GENESIS 1:1-3.

In the beginning God (Allah) created the heavens and the earth. Now the earth was formless and empty, darkness was over the surface of the deep, and the Spirit (Al-Ruwh) of God (Allah) was hovering over the waters. And God (Allah) said, "Let there be light," and there was light.

As far as an attribute revealed in this passage, we see that Allah is eternal—without beginning or end. Before anything else in the universe existed, Allah was there. Everything was created by and through Allah's Word. In Genesis 2, Allah gives us a tiny glimpse into the garden, a Paradise where Adam and Hawa (Eve in English) lived. But Genesis 3 reveals the first sin of humankind, which originated terrible sufferings for humans and indeed for all of creation.

PLEASE TURN TO AND READ GENESIS 3:22–24.

And the Lord God said, "The man has now become like one of us, knowing good and evil. He must not be allowed to reach out his hand and take also from the tree of life and eat and live forever." So the Lord God banished him from the Garden of Eden to work the ground from which he had been taken. After he drove the man out, he placed on the east side of the Garden of Eden cherubim and a flaming sword flashing back and forth to guard the way to the tree of life.

Then through the rest of the Holy Bible, Allah reveals the One and only Way humankind can be restored into Paradise with Allah.

Allah finishes Holy Scriptures in the last book of the Holy Bible, Revelation, with a prophecy that includes Judgment Day, and the restoration of humankind into Paradise.

PLEASE TURN TO AND READ REVELATION 22:12–14.

Look, I am coming soon! My reward is with me, and I will give to each person according to what they have done. I am the Alpha and the Omega, the First and the Last, the Beginning and the End. Blessed are those who wash their robes, that they may have the right to the tree of life and may go through the gates into the city.

Notes

- Genesis (*Taqueen* in Arabic) was Allah-breathed through nabi Musa (the prophet Moses in English) around 3,425 years ago.
- Revelation was Allah-breathed through John around 1,925 years ago.

Allah *wants* to welcome everyone into Paradise. He has a place prepared for you and for me!

Please pause here and ponder what you've read.

- Explain the passages in your own words as if you were sharing it with someone else.
- Explain how the passages make you think or feel and why.
- What do the passages tell you about Allah?
- What do the passages tell you about you and your relationship with Allah?
- What action do you think Allah wants from you according to these passages?
- As a result, create an "I will ..." statement to obey Allah according to these passages.

What Else Does Allah Reveal about Himself in the Holy Bible?

We will look at some aspects of Allah that are vital to discovering and understanding Allah's One Way back to Paradise: His supremacy, His righteousness as judge, and His infinite love and faithfulness. Let's start by looking at Allah's supremacy.

There Is Only One Allah!

Allah affirms throughout the Holy Bible that there is only one Allah/God. Please turn to and read the following four passages:

DEUTERONOMY 4:39

"Acknowledge and take to heart this day that the Lord is God in heaven above and on the earth below. There is no other."

DEUTERONOMY 32:39A

"See now that I myself am He! There is no god besides me ... "

ISAIAH 43:10–11

"You are my witnesses," declares the Lord, "and my servant whom I have chosen, so that you may know and believe me and understand that I am He. Before me no god was formed, nor will there be one after me. I, even I, am the Lord, and apart from me there is no Savior."

1 CORINTHIANS 8:4

So then, about eating food sacrificed to idols: We know that "An idol is nothing at all in the world" and that "There is no God but one."

> **Note**
> - 1 Corinthians was Allah-breathed through the Apostle Paul around 1,965 years ago.

Allah Is the Righteous Judge

Allah affirms throughout the Holy Bible that He is the one and only Judge. Please turn to and read the following five examples:

PSALM 7:11A

God (Allah) is a righteous Judge . . .

PSALM 50:6

And the heavens proclaim his righteousness, for He is a God (Allah) of justice.

PSALM 89:34

I will not violate my covenant or alter what my lips have uttered.

ISAIAH 33:22

For the Lord is our judge, the Lord is our lawgiver, the Lord is our king; it is He who will save us.

JAMES 4:12

There is only one Lawgiver and Judge, the one who is able to save and destroy. But you—who are you to judge your neighbor?

> **Note**
> - James was Allah-breathed through James around 1,970 years ago.

Please pause here and consider what you've read.

- Explain the passages in your own words as if you were sharing it with someone else.
- Explain how the passages make you think or feel and why.
- What do the passages tell you about Allah?
- What do the passages tell you about you and your relationship with Allah?
- What action do you think Allah wants from you according to these passages?
- As a result, create an "I will . . ." statement to obey Allah according to these passages.

Allah Is Infinite in His Love and Faithfulness

Throughout the Holy Bible, Infinite Allah reveals characteristics of Himself. His attributes of love and compassion are essential for us to recognize as we seek to understand and choose to follow His One Way to Paradise with Him. Please turn to and read the following seven Holy passages:

EXODUS 34:6

And He passed in front of Moses (Musa in Arabic), proclaiming, "The Lord, the Lord, the compassionate and gracious God, slow to anger, abounding in love and faithfulness . . ."

NUMBERS 14:18A

The Lord is slow to anger, abounding in love and forgiving sin and rebellion. Yet he does not leave the guilty unpunished . . .

DEUTERONOMY 32:4

"He is the Rock, his works are perfect, and all his ways are just. A faithful God who does no wrong, upright and just is he."

Allah's Story and Revelations about Himself

PSALM 68:5

A father to the fatherless, a defender of widows, is God (Allah) in his holy dwelling.

PSALM 85:9-10

Surely his salvation is near those who fear him, that his glory may dwell in our land. Love and faithfulness meet together, righteousness and peace kiss each other.

1 PETER 1:15-16

But just as He who called you is holy, so be holy in all you do; for it is written: "Be holy, because I am holy."

1 JOHN 4:8

Whoever does not love does not know God (Allah), because God (Allah) is love.

Notes

- Exodus was Allah-breathed through nabi Musa (the prophet Moses in English) around 3,425 years ago.
- Numbers was also Allah-breathed through nabi Musa around 3,425 years ago.
- 1 Peter was Allah-breathed through Peter around 1,955 years ago.
- 1 John was Allah-breathed through John around 1,925 years ago.

Please pause here and ponder what you've read.

- Explain the passages in your own words as if you were sharing it with someone else.
- Explain how the passages make you think or feel and why.

- What do the passages tell you about Allah?
- What do the passages tell you about you and your relationship with Allah?
- What action do you think Allah wants from you according to these passages?
- As a result, create an "I will..." statement to obey Allah according to these passages.

Chapter Conclusion

Through the Holy Scriptures that we reviewed in this chapter, Allah reveals Himself as the infinitely powerful Creator, the One and only Allah, Savior, King, Lawgiver, Judge, Father, Love, the Alpha and the Omega, the First and the Last, the Beginning and the End.

Allah also shows us in His Word that He is holy and has in perfect balance the traits of compassion, patience, love, faithfulness, justice (He will not leave sins unpunished), righteousness (He does no wrong), forgiveness, and peace.

Allah began the story of the Holy Bible in Genesis, about 3,500 years ago, by revealing that in his infinite wisdom and power, He spoke, and through His Word everything was created. Humans enjoyed perfect life in Paradise with all-loving Allah. When humans sinned, bringing suffering, death, and destruction into the world, He expelled humans from Paradise, all the while working His plan of eternal redemption.

Allah ends the story of the Holy Bible in the book of Revelation, about 1,925 years ago, revealing the conditional good news that when He comes in the end, "those who wash their robes . . . may have the right to the tree of life and may go through the gates into" Paradise (Rev. 22:14). Access to the tree of life (which, within the context of the Holy Bible, refers to eternal life) is limited only to "those who wash their robes." We'll explore the meaning of this in future chapters.

The Holy Bible is rich with insight about Allah, but what we have covered here gives us an overview of how humankind was separated from Him and expelled from Paradise—and that He has a Way by which we are restored into Paradise.

I am thrilled to continue this exciting journey with you. Let us close this session with prayer.

Will You Pray That Allah Will Reveal the Truth to You about His Word?

- What specific requests do you have for Allah now?
- If you have a Christian friend, then ask him or her to pray with you in the name of Jesus.
- If you do not know or have access to a Christian near you, then please contact us with your specific prayer request (pray@WordofAllah.org).

Be specific with any need or issue that Allah can do for you today, even if it is miraculous. It does not mean that Allah will perform a physical miracle for you. The greatest miracle Allah desires for you is eternal life in Paradise, and He has already accomplished that. In this book we study how you can have this greatest miracle from Allah. It is already yours if you choose it.

Jesus Heals a Paralytic

LUKE 5:17-26

One day Jesus was teaching, and Pharisees and teachers of the law were sitting there. They had come from every village of Galilee and from Judea and Jerusalem. And the power of the Lord was with Jesus to heal the sick. Some men came carrying a paralyzed man on a mat and tried to take him into the house to lay him before Jesus. When they could not find a way to do this because of the crowd, they went up on the roof and lowered him on his mat through the tiles into the middle of the crowd, right in front of Jesus.

When Jesus saw their faith, he said, "Friend, your sins are forgiven."

The Pharisees and the teachers of the law began thinking to themselves, "Who is this fellow who speaks blasphemy? Who can forgive sins but God (Allah) alone?"

Jesus knew what they were thinking and asked, "Why are you thinking these things in your hearts? Which is easier: to say, 'Your sins are forgiven,' or to say, 'Get up and walk'? But I want you to know that the Son of Man has authority on earth to forgive sins." So he said to the paralyzed man, "I tell you, get up, take your mat and go home."

Immediately he stood up in front of them, took what he had been lying on and went home praising God (Allah). Everyone was amazed and gave praise to God (Allah). They were filled with awe and said, "We have seen remarkable things today."

Jesus Heals a Leper

LUKE 5:12-16

While Jesus was in one of the towns, a man came along who was covered with leprosy. When he saw Jesus, he fell with his face to the ground and begged him, "Lord, if you are willing, you can make me clean."

Jesus reached out his hand and touched the man. "I am willing," he said. "Be clean!" and immediately the leprosy left him.

Then Jesus ordered him, "Don't tell anyone, but go, show yourself to the priest and offer the sacrifices that Moses commanded for your cleansing, as a testimony to them."

Yet the news about him spread all the more, so that crowds of people came to hear him and to be healed of their sicknesses. But Jesus often withdrew to lonely places and prayed.

Non-Christian Healed from Deformed Arm

One of my sons spends time regularly with non-Christians, telling them about Jesus and praying for them in the name of Jesus. One warm day, he went with one of his Christian friends, Jim, to do that together at a place popular with college students.

Jim asked two young men walking by if he could pray for them about something. One of them said to Jim, "Look at my arm. The skin and arm look deformed and ugly. Don't worry; it is not contagious. It's always been like this. I don't believe in God, but if you want to pray for it, why not, do it."

Jim and my son put their hands on his arm and prayed to God to reveal Himself to the student by healing his arm " . . . in the name of Jesus. Amen!"

Immediately, while Jim, my son, the non-Christian student, and his friend were looking at his deformed and ugly arm, it was instantly healed and transformed, looking healthy and strong. The young man's arm and body were shaking; he looked afraid and amazed at the same time, and tears streamed down his face. Meanwhile, he repeatedly looked from Jim and my son and then back to his arm Then he and his friend quickly ran away without saying a word.

Praising Allah's Abundant Goodness and Love

PSALM 103

Praise the Lord, my soul; all my inmost being, praise his holy name.

Praise the Lord, my soul, and forget not all his benefits—

Who forgives all your sins and heals all your diseases,

Who redeems your life from the pit and crowns you with love and compassion,

Who satisfies your desires with good things so that your youth is renewed like the eagle's.

The Lord works righteousness and justice for all the oppressed.

He made known his ways to Moses, his deeds to the people of Israel:

The Lord is compassionate and gracious, slow to anger, abounding in love.

He will not always accuse, nor will he harbor his anger forever;

He does not treat us as our sins deserve or repay us according to our iniquities.

For as high as the heavens are above the earth, so great is his love for those who fear him;

As far as the east is from the west, so far has he removed our transgressions from us.

As a father has compassion on his children, so the Lord has compassion on those who fear him;

For he knows how we are formed, he remembers that we are dust.

The life of mortals is like grass, they flourish like a flower of the field;

The wind blows over it and it is gone, and its place remembers it no more.

But from everlasting to everlasting the Lord's love is with those who fear him, and his righteousness with their children's children—

With those who keep his covenant and remember to obey his precepts.

The Lord has established his throne in heaven, and his kingdom rules over all.

Praise the Lord, you his angels, you mighty ones who do his bidding, who obey his word.

Praise the Lord, all his heavenly hosts, you his servants who do his will.

Praise the Lord, all his works everywhere in his dominion. Praise the Lord, my soul.

Chapter Four

Allah's Creation

Let us begin with a prayer:

We pray that the Holy Spirit of Allah will fill us to reveal, guide, and teach us the truth as we discover Allah's story and revelations in the Holy Bible. In Jesus's name, amen!

*I*n the previous chapter, we very briefly looked at the story of creation. In this chapter, we will take a closer look at the account of how Allah created humankind, at His purpose for you and me, and how things were for humankind in Paradise.

Please begin this study by reading Genesis chapters 1 and 2.

Now that you have read the two chapters, let's divide the material into smaller sections so we can better comprehend Allah's revelations.

GENESIS 1:1–5

In the beginning God (Allah) created the heavens and the earth. Now the earth was formless and empty, darkness was over the surface of the deep, and the Spirit of God (Allah) was hovering over the waters. And God (Allah) said, "Let there be light," and there was light. God (Allah) saw that the light was good, and he separated the light from the darkness. God (Allah) called the light "day," and the darkness he called "night." And there was evening, and there was morning—the first day.

Allah creates everything through His Word. Please pause to meditate on what this reveals to you about Allah and His Word.

GENESIS 1:6–25

And God (Allah) said, "Let there be a vault between the waters to separate water from water." So God (Allah) made the vault and separated the water under the vault from the water above it. And it was so. God (Allah) called the vault "sky." And there was evening, and there was morning—the second day.

And God (Allah) said, "Let the water under the sky be gathered to one place, and let dry ground appear." And it was so. God (Allah) called the dry ground "land," and the gathered waters he called "seas." And God (Allah) saw that it was good.

Then God (Allah) said, "Let the land produce vegetation: seed-bearing plants, and trees on the land that bear fruit with seed in it, according to their various kinds." And it was so. The land produced vegetation: plants bearing seed according to their kinds and trees bearing fruit with seed in it according to their kinds. And God (Allah) saw that it was good. And there was evening, and there was morning—the third day.

And God (Allah) said, "Let there be lights in the vault of the sky to separate the day from the night, and let them serve as signs to mark sacred times, and days and years, and let them be lights in the vault of the sky to give light on the earth." And it was so. God (Allah) made two great lights—the greater light to govern the day and the lesser light to govern the night. He also made the stars. God (Allah) set them in the vault of the sky to give light on the earth, to govern the day and the night, and to separate light from darkness. And God (Allah) saw that it was good. And there was evening, and there was morning—the fourth day.

And God (Allah) said, "Let the water teem with living creatures, and let birds fly above the earth across the vault of the sky." So God (Allah) created the great creatures of the sea and every living thing with which the water teems and that moves about on it, according to their kinds, and every winged bird according to its kind. And God (Allah) saw that it was good. God (Allah) blessed them and said, "Be fruitful and increase in number and fill the water in the seas, and let the birds increase on the earth." And there was evening, and there was morning—the fifth day.

And God (Allah) said, "Let the land produce living creatures according to their kinds: the livestock, the creatures that move along the ground, and the wild animals, each according to its kind." And it was so. God (Allah) made the wild animals according to their kinds, the livestock according to their kinds, and all the creatures that move along the ground according to their kinds. And God (Allah) saw that it was good.

Here are some thoughts on my understanding of this summary of Allah's creation story.

Allah divides . . .

Day 1	Day 2	Day 3
. . . day and night	. . . water and heaven	. . . land and sea

Allah fills . . .

Day 4	Day 5	Day 6
. . . day and night with lights	. . . water and air with life	. . . land and sea with life

> **Questions**
> - What does Allah say about His work after each day?
> - To me, the above verses reveal that Allah is good, caring, perfect, beautiful, and orderly. What do these verses reveal to you?

Creation of Humankind

GENESIS 1:26–27

Then God (Allah) said, "Let us make mankind in our image, in our likeness, so that they may rule over the fish in the sea and the birds in the sky, over the livestock and all the wild animals, and over all the creatures that move along the ground. So God (Allah) created mankind in his own image, in the image of God (Allah) he created them; male and female he created them.

> **Questions**
> - How many times in these verses does Allah emphasize that He created mankind in His image?
> - What does Allah's emphasis imply to you?

Allah values humankind, male and female, and He created you and me in His image. The first time I read those verses I did not know what that meant. As I continued to study the Holy Bible, I saw that Allah uses many metaphors or figures of speech to communicate difficult truths to us in ways and language we may understand. We do not take a figure of speech like this literally.

Allah gave humankind some abilities that He did not give to other created beings. Here are a few examples that demonstrate what it means to be created in the image of Allah:

- Humankind can think and reason (Allah does), not merely go by instinct.
- Humankind can distinguish between good and evil (Allah does).
- Humankind can have a unique relationship with Allah.
- Humankind share personal characteristics in common with Allah, like the ones we studied in chapter three of this book: love, compassion, faithfulness, etc.

Allah's Two-fold Purpose for Humankind

GENESIS 1:28–31

God (Allah) blessed them and said to them, "Be fruitful and increase in number; fill the earth and subdue it. Rule over the fish in the sea and the birds in the sky and over every living creature that moves on the ground. Then God (Allah) said, "I give you every seed-bearing plant on the face of the whole earth and every tree that has fruit with seed in it. They will be yours for food. And to all the beasts of the earth—everything that has the breath of life in it—I give every green plant for food." And it was so. God (Allah) saw all that he had made, and it was very good. And there was evening, and there was morning—the sixth day.

GENESIS 2:15

The Lord God (Allah) took the man and put him in the Garden of Eden to work it and take care of it.

Question

- What do these verses imply as the two-fold purpose of humankind?

Humankind was created to take care of creation. In this way, humankind is in the image of the Creator in that Allah is the Supreme Ruler who rules over everything, and humankind was to rule (work and take care of) over Allah's Paradise.

Please pause here and ponder what you've read.
- Explain the passages in your own words as if you were sharing it with someone else.
- Explain how the passages make you think or feel and why.
- What do the passages tell you about Allah?
- What do the passages tell you about you and your relationship with Allah?
- What action do you think Allah wants from you according to these passages?
- As a result, create an "I will . . ." statement to obey Allah according to these passages.

Sabbath Rest

GENESIS 2:1–3

Thus the heavens and the earth were completed in all their vast array. By the seventh day God (Allah) had finished the work he had been doing; so on the seventh day he rested from all his work. Then God (Allah) blessed the seventh day and made it holy, because on it he rested from all the work of creating that he had done.

When Allah finished the work of creation, He blessed the seventh day as one of rest.

> **PLEASE TURN TO AND READ ISAIAH 40:28.**
> *Do you not know? Have you not heard? The Lord is the everlasting God (Allah), the Creator of the ends of the earth. He will not grow tired or weary, and his understanding no one can fathom.*

Allah never grows tired, but He knows that we do! So Allah created a day of rest for us so that we can stop during our busy lives and intentionally remember Him and all He has done as we focus on worshipping and spending time with Him.

Knowledge of Good and Evil

> **GENESIS 2:16–17**
> *And the Lord God (Allah) commanded the man, "You are free to eat from any tree in the garden; but you must not eat from the tree of the knowledge of good and evil, for when you eat from it you will certainly die."*

Questions

- How many trees were available for mankind to eat from in the Garden of Eden?
- How many trees was humankind not allowed to eat from?
- What does that communicate about Allah's rules?

Allah does not reveal in the Holy Bible how many trees were available for mankind to eat from in the Garden of Eden, but the verses in Genesis 1 and 2 indicate there were plenty! Allah restricted humankind from only one tree, representing the knowledge of good and evil. To me, this reveals that Allah's commandment here is not harsh or narrow. Sometimes it appears to humans as if Allah's rules are restrictive, when in reality they are intended to protect and benefit us.

> **Question**
>
> - Why would Allah forbid humankind to eat from the tree of the knowledge of good and evil?

Allah reveals throughout the Holy Bible that He intended man to know only goodness. Allah's goodness is infinitely greater than anything and everything else! Allah did not want humankind to know evil, which carries with it shame, pain, suffering, and death.

Allah did not need to create humans. Out of His infinite and perfect love, He chose to create and love humans. But, as in human relationships, true love cannot be forced. So Allah created humans with the freedom and ability to choose whether to believe, trust, depend on, and love Allah in return. Allah warned humankind of the responsibility that comes with that freedom and ability to choose. The choice we make can result in life or death!

Having the freedom to choose between life and death may seem like a heavy one. Many people fear or ignore the responsibility to choose. In Deuteronomy 30:11–14, however, Allah tells us that He has made the choice simple for us. He isn't trying to trick or trap us, so He speaks plainly about His Way.

Please turn to and read Deuteronomy 30:11–14 and then let's consider these two particular phrases:

"Now what I am commanding you today is not too difficult for you or beyond your reach..." (v. 11)

"No, the word is very near you; it is in your mouth and in your heart so you may obey it." (v. 14)

Allah's command to Adam and Hawa in Genesis 2:16–17 was simple to keep. Allah and His Word were right there with them. Allah's Word continues to be close to you and me today. Allah makes it available to each of us through the Holy Bible.

> **PLEASE TURN TO AND READ DEUTERONOMY 30:15–20.**
>
> *See, I set before you today life and prosperity, death and destruction. For I command you today to love the Lord your God, to walk in obedience to him, and to keep his commands, decrees and laws; then you will live and increase, and the Lord your God will bless you in the land you are entering to possess.*
>
> *But if your heart turns away and you are not obedient, and if you are drawn away to bow down to other gods and worship them, I declare to you this day that you will certainly be destroyed. You will not live long in the land you are crossing the Jordan to enter and possess.*
>
> *. . . I have set before you life and death, blessings and curses. Now choose life, so that you and your children may live and that you may love the Lord your God, listen to his voice, and hold fast to him. For the Lord is your life . . . .*

Allah's commands, promises, warnings, and choices in Deuteronomy are around 2,500 years after the ones He gave in Genesis 2:16–17. Allah gave a consistent message to humankind throughout history, and He continues to give them to you and me today through His Word. Allah desired for Adam and Hawa—and you and me—to make the choice that leads to eternal life with Him in Paradise.

Let us resume the study of Allah's revelation about creation and life in Paradise in Genesis 2.

GENESIS 2:18–25

The Lord God (Allah) said, "It is not good for the man to be alone. I will make a helper suitable for him." Now the Lord God (Allah) had formed out of the ground all the wild animals and all the birds in the sky. He brought them to the man to see what he would name them; and whatever the man called each living creature, that was its name. So the man gave names to all the livestock in the sky and all the wild animals.

But for Adam no suitable helper was found. So the Lord God (Allah) caused the man to fall into a deep sleep; and while he was sleeping, he took one of the man's ribs and then closed up the place with flesh. Then the Lord God (Allah) made a woman from the rib he had taken out of the man, and he brought her to the man. The man said, "This is now bone of my bones and flesh of my flesh; she shall be called 'woman,' for she was taken out of man."

That is why a man leaves his father and mother and is united to his wife, and they become one flesh. Adam and his wife were both naked, and they felt no shame.

There were no feelings of shame before Adam and Eve sinned. Shame is a consequence of sin.

Please pause here and ponder what you've read.

- Explain the above passages from Genesis chapter two in your own words as if you were sharing them with someone else.
- Explain how the passages make you think or feel and why.
- What do the passages tell you about Allah?
- What do the passages tell you about you and your relationship with Allah?

- What action do you think Allah wants from you according to these passages?
- As a result, create an "I will..." statement to obey Allah according to these passages.

Chapter Conclusion

In this chapter of the Holy Scriptures that we reviewed, I saw Allah as being thoroughly good, loving, and caring towards humankind, creating us in an amazing and beautiful way. Allah created humankind for a perfect relationship with Him, for a perfect life, with a perfect body, in perfect surroundings, with no sin, no shame, no pain, and no disease.

Allah created humankind in the image of Allah. In Paradise, humankind had, and can once again, have a close fellowship with Allah. Allah loves you, values you, and wants to have a close relationship with you. Allah first created light and brought everything into perfect order. Allah can brighten up any darkness in your life today.

As for me, as I shared with you earlier, I was full of sin, and did not choose to believe, trust, depend on, or love Allah. After I chose to believe, trust, and depend on Allah, Jesus transformed my heart, removing anger and hate, and replacing it with love for Allah, Muslims, and toward humankind created in His image.

How about you?

How would you describe your personal relationship with Allah?

Will you choose to believe, trust, depend on, and love Allah in the only true and holy Way acceptable to Him according to His revelation in the Holy Bible?

Insha'Allah you and I will become spiritual siblings.

Will You Pray That Allah Will Reveal the Truth to You about His Word?

- What specific requests do you have for Allah now?
- If you have a Christian friend, then ask him or her to pray with you in the name of Jesus.
- If you do not know or have access to a Christian near you, then please contact us with your specific prayer request (pray@WordofAllah.org).

Be specific with any need or issue that Allah can do for you today, even if it is miraculous. It does not mean that Allah will perform a physical miracle for you. The greatest miracle Allah desires for you is eternal life in Paradise, and He has already accomplished that. In this book we study how you can have this greatest miracle from Allah. It is already yours if you choose it.

Jesus Calms a Storm

MARK 4:35-41

That day when evening came, he said to his disciples, "Let us go over to the other side." Leaving the crowd behind, they took him along, just as he was, in the boat. There were also other boats with him. A furious squall came up, and the waves broke over the boat, so that it was nearly swamped. Jesus was in the stern, sleeping on a cushion. The disciples woke him and said to him, "Teacher, don't you care if we drown?"

He got up, rebuked the wind and said to the waves, "Quiet! Be still!" Then the wind died down and it was completely calm. He said to his disciples, "Why are you so afraid? Do you still have no faith?"

They were terrified and asked each other, "Who is this? Even the wind and the waves obey him!"

Woman Healed!

MARK 5:21-34

When Jesus had again crossed over by boat to the other side of the lake, a large crowd gathered around him while he was by the lake. Then one of the synagogue leaders, named Jairus, came, and when he saw Jesus, he fell at his feet. He pleaded earnestly with him, "My little daughter is dying. Please come and put your hands on her so that she will be healed and live." So Jesus went with him.

A large crowd followed and pressed around him. And a woman was there who had been subject to bleeding for twelve years. She had suffered a great deal under the care of many doctors and had spent all she had, yet instead of getting better she grew worse. When she heard about Jesus, she came up behind him in the crowd and touched his cloak, because she thought, "If I just touch his clothes, I will be healed."

Immediately her bleeding stopped and she felt in her body that she was freed from her suffering. At once Jesus realized that power had gone out from him. He turned around in the crowd and asked, "Who touched my clothes?"

"You see the people crowding against you," his disciples answered, "and yet you can ask, 'Who touched me?'"

But Jesus kept looking around to see who had done it. Then the woman, knowing what had happened to her, came and fell at his feet and, trembling with fear, told him the whole truth. He said to her, "Daughter, your faith has healed you. Go in peace and be freed from your suffering."

Jesus Raises Dead Girl

MARK 5:35–42

While Jesus was still speaking, some people came from the house of Jairus, the synagogue leader. "Your daughter is dead," they said. "Why bother the teacher anymore?" Overhearing what they said, Jesus told him, "Don't be afraid; just believe."

He did not let anyone follow him except Peter, James, and John the brother of James. When they came to the home of the synagogue leader, Jesus saw a commotion, with people crying and wailing loudly. He went in and said to them, "Why all this commotion and wailing? The child is not dead but asleep." But they laughed at him.

After he put them all out, he took the child's father and mother and the disciples who were with him, and went in where the child was. He took her by the hand and said to her, "Talitha koum!" (which means "Little girl, I say to you, get up!"). Immediately the girl stood up and began to walk around (she was twelve years old). At this they were completely astonished.

How Allah Saved My Life—Part One

For a variety of reasons, I wanted to end my life during my early forties. At the time, I was suffering physically from several health conditions, including debilitating pain in my back. The pain was so excruciating that I was unable to work and provide financially for my family.

At one point, due to this back condition, I lay in bed for several days. I could not even go to the bathroom, needing someone to help me while I lay in bed. I felt ashamed—as if I were no longer a "man" but a dependent child.

At that point in my life, I believed in Allah and His One and only Way back to Paradise. As I lay in bed, I prayed non-stop, in the name of Jesus. I pleaded with Allah to heal me, but He did not. I cried and prayed that Allah would talk with me, tell me anything, give me hope, but after three days of all the prayers, I did not hear anything from Allah. I lost all hope.

My family was in such severe financial trouble that we were about to lose our home. As I lay in bed unable to work, I reasoned that if I could not provide financially for my family while living, I could do so through the life insurance money they would get in the event of my death. Desperate and depressed, I planned to end my life the following morning while home alone.

That night I prayed to Allah to forgive me for what I was about to do in the morning. Then I heard a voice in my head say, "Look." I did not know whose voice it was, nor did I understand what this voice wanted me to look at. But the voice kept repeating, "Look," louder and louder. At that point I felt overwhelmed by emotion and wondered if it was Allah speaking to me. If so, it would have been the first time ever in my life.

I asked, "Lord, if it is you, please tell me. Also, what do you want me to look at?" I heard the voice in my head say, "Look outside the window." I turned my head on the bed toward the window with the open curtain next to the bed. I could not see anything; it was pitch black outside. I said, "I am looking, but I do not see anything."

"Look and focus," the voice said. I kept staring out the window, squinting my eyes and focusing my gaze. I began to see stars twinkling in the night skies. The more I focused and gazed, the more stars I saw, looking bigger and brighter. Then the voice said, "In your darkest hour is when you can look into my light without going blind. Get up!"

"But I cannot get up," I said, "my back will not let me."

"Get up!" the voice said.

"Then do what?" I said, "My family would still be better off financially if I am dead."

Then I heard these words: *"Do not worry, saying, 'What shall we eat?' or 'What shall we drink?' or 'What shall we wear?' For the pagans run after all these things, and your heavenly Father knows that you need them. But seek first his kingdom and his righteousness, and all these things will be given to you as well. Therefore do not worry about tomorrow, for tomorrow will worry about itself. Each day has enough trouble of its own."*

That's when I knew it was Jesus speaking to me. The conversation ended with His words as recorded in the Holy Bible, Matthew 6:31–34. For the first time in such a long time, I felt a ray of hope.

Eventually, I was able to get up and get back to work. We did not lose our house, and we just barely survived financially. My overall struggles continued, but that night, Jesus saved my life.

Allah's Majesty

PSALM 8

Lord, our Lord, how majestic is your name in all the earth! You have set your glory in the heavens.

Through the praise of children and infants you have established a stronghold against your enemies, to silence the foe and the avenger.

When I consider your heavens, the work of your fingers, the moon and the stars, which you have set in place,

What is mankind that you are mindful of them, human beings that you care for them?

You have made them a little lower than the angels and crowned them with glory and honor.

You made them rulers over the works of your hands; you put everything under their feet:

All flocks and herds, and animals of the wild,

The birds in the sky, and the fish in the sea, all that swim the paths of the seas.

Lord, our Lord, how majestic is your name in all the earth!

Chapter Five

Sin and Shame

As always, let us begin with a prayer:
We pray that the Holy Spirit of Allah will fill us to reveal, guide, and teach us the truth as we discover Allah's Word and revelations in the Holy Bible. In Jesus's name, amen!

With His Word, Allah created a beautiful Paradise. With His great love, He created humans in His image and gave them that perfect place to live in and to care for and charged them to be fruitful and multiply. Allah wanted Adam and Hawa to enjoy this place, and it was here that He walked with them in the cool of the day. Can you imagine what that must have been like?

Adam and Hawa experienced a perfect relationship of peace with Allah and companionship with one another. They lived without fear and did not even know what shame was—until sin entered the story. In this chapter we will see the devastating impact that sin and shame have had on every human being who has ever lived, including you and me. As we review Allah's revelation of the story of humankind being expelled from Paradise, we will see how sin severed the close relationship humanity had with the holy and righteous Creator, but we will also see that Allah still loves humankind despite our sin and the shame we bear.

Right from the start of life, Allah provided what we needed. And even when sin and shame covered humankind, Allah continued to provide for us. As we will read together in the Holy Bible, from the beginning, Allah had a plan—a holy, righteous, and complete Way for you and me to return to eternal Paradise and peace with Allah.

Before we begin, please read Genesis 3.

Now, let us divide the chapter into smaller sections so we can better comprehend Allah's revelation.

Sin Enters the World

GENESIS 3:1–6

Now the serpent was more crafty than any of the wild animals the Lord God had made. He said to the woman, "Did God (Allah) really say, 'You must not eat from any tree in the garden'?"

The woman said to the serpent, "We may eat fruit from the trees in the garden, but God (Allah) did say, 'You must not eat fruit from the tree that is in the middle of the garden, and you must not touch it, or you will die.'"

"You will not certainly die," the serpent said to the woman. "For God (Allah) knows that when you eat from it your eyes will be opened, and you will be like God (Allah), knowing good and evil."

When the woman saw that the fruit of the tree was good for food and pleasing to the eye, and also desirable for gaining wisdom, she took some and ate it. She also gave some to her husband, who was with her, and he ate it.

> **Question**
> - Who is the serpent?

Through my journey of reading and studying the Holy Bible, I discovered that Allah uses His Word to help us understand the revelations He provides within it. By that I mean that we can often find answers to our questions about the Scriptures by reading elsewhere within the Holy Bible. I found the answer to this particular question about the serpent in Revelation (the last book of the Holy Bible). Let's look at a few verses together.

REVELATION 12:9

The great dragon was hurled down—that ancient serpent called the devil, or Satan (Iblis or Sheetan in Arabic), who leads the whole world astray. He was hurled to the earth, and his angels with him.

REVELATION 20:2

He seized the dragon, that ancient serpent, who is the devil, or Satan, and bound him for a thousand years.

> **Question**
> - What is Satan's strategy in Genesis 3:1–6?

In my own life experiences and throughout all of history, I noticed that there are five main tactics that Satan uses to bring evil into our lives:

1. **He encourages us to doubt Allah's Word.** He does this with Hawa in Genesis 3:1 when he says, "Did God (Allah) really say . . . ?"
2. **He twists Allah's Word to increase our burdens.** As he invited Hawa to doubt, he also twisted Allah's command by stating it

inaccurately: "*You must not eat from any tree in the garden.*" In reality, Allah actually only commanded them to abstain from one specific tree in Genesis 2:17: "*but you must not eat from the tree of the knowledge of good and evil.*"

3. **He lies.** In Genesis 3:4–5, Satan assures Hawa that she would be just fine—even better, in fact—if she disobeyed Allah: "*You will not surely die . . . you will be like God (Allah).*"

4. **Satan uses half-truths.** Look at how he tempts Hawa in Genesis 3:5: "*. . . when you eat of it your eyes will be opened . . .*" That part was true, but he left out the consequence that disobeying Allah would carry.

5. **He invites us to mistrust Allah and His motives.** In Genesis 3:5, Satan tells Hawa, "*For God (Allah) knows that when you eat from it your eyes will be opened, and you will be like God (Allah), knowing good and evil.*" It is as if the serpent were saying, "Allah doesn't want what is best for you; He is keeping the good stuff for Himself."

The First Result of Sin

In Genesis 2:25, we read that "*Adam and his wife were both naked, and they felt no shame.*" Before they sinned, they knew nothing of shame.

But things changed when they disobeyed Allah. In Genesis 3:7, after Adam and Hawa sinned, we read that "*Then the eyes of both of them were opened, and they realized they were naked; so they sewed fig leaves together and made coverings for themselves.*"

Questions

- What is the first result of sin?
- What is the first thing humans do after sin?
- Shame comes with sin. Adam and Hawa immediately tried to cover their sin and shame and they hid from Allah.
- How has shame impacted your life? Your relationships with others? Your relationship with Allah?

The Second Result of Sin

GENESIS 3:8–10

Then the man and his wife heard the sound of the Lord God as he was walking in the garden in the cool of the day, and they hid from the Lord God among the trees of the garden. But the Lord God called to the man, "Where are you?" He answered, "I heard you in the garden, and I was afraid because I was naked; so I hid."

Questions

- What do you observe is the second result of sin?
- What was Allah's first action after humankind sinned?

Allah is most holy. Before sin, humans lived in His presence in Paradise. But when Adam and Hawa sinned, just like all humans since, they became impure and filled with shame. They were rightfully afraid to be in the presence of holy Allah.

From the beginning, however, despite sin and shame, Allah initiates a relationship with us. He calls for us, just as He did to Adam and Hawa. Allah, who is infinite love, reveals throughout the Holy Bible that He desires a relationship with us.

The Blame Game

GENESIS 3:11-13

And he said, "Who told you that you were naked? Have you eaten from the tree that I commanded you not to eat from?" The man said, "The woman you put here with me—she gave me some fruit from the tree, and I ate it." Then the Lord God said to the woman, "What is this you have done?" The woman said, "The serpent deceived me, and I ate."

Question

- What is typically the first reaction humans have after being confronted with their sin?

Like most humans, I notice that I am sometimes guilty of what Adam initially did, which is to indirectly blame Allah for sin by saying to Allah: "The woman *you* put here with me . . . "

Allah's Words to Iblis

GENESIS 3:14-15

So the Lord God said to the serpent, "Because you have done this, cursed are you above all livestock and all wild animals! You will crawl on your belly and you will eat dust all the days of your life. And I will put enmity between you and the woman, and between your offspring and hers; he will crush your head, and you will strike his heel."

In Genesis 3:15, Allah gives the very first prophecy (prediction) in the Holy Bible, hinting at His One Way back to Paradise. Allah's prophecy is directed to Iblis in connection to the offspring of the woman: *"he will crush your head, and you will strike his heel."* In context, Allah is saying that an offspring of Hawa will crush Iblis's head, while Iblis will bruise his heel.

It is here in Genesis 3:15, that Allah begins to reveal His One Way to restoring relationship with humanity. A little at a time, over a period of more than 1,500 years, Allah continued to reveal His plan for salvation through dozens of prophets on three different continents. As you continue to read His Word, you will discover how Allah's plan impacts every human, including you and me. Allah, in His infinite and perfect wisdom, chose to reveal His Way through prophecy and story. As I studied Allah's revelations through the Holy Bible, His truth became abundantly clear. I pray that Allah's Holy Spirit will also make it clear to you.

The Third Result of Sin

GENESIS 3:16-18

To the woman he said, "I will make your pains in childbearing very severe; with painful labor you will give birth to children. Your desire will be for your husband, and he will rule over you."

To Adam he said, "Because you listened to your wife and ate fruit from the tree about which I commanded you, 'You must not eat from it,' cursed is the ground because of you; through painful toil you will eat food from it all the days of your life. It will produce thorns and thistles for you, and you will eat the plants of the field."

The Fourth Result of Sin

> GENESIS 3:19
> *By the sweat of your brow you will eat your food until you return to the ground, since from it you were taken; for dust you are and to dust you will return.*

The Provision with the First Sacrifice

> GENESIS 3:20-21
> *Adam named his wife Eve (Hawa), because she would become the mother of all the living. The Lord God (Allah) made garments of skin for Adam and his wife and clothed them.*

As we read earlier in Genesis 3:7, humankind tried to cover their nakedness and shame inadequately with fig leaves. Out of His love, Allah provides them with a more adequate covering, clothes from skin, which means it required the first death after sin, the sacrifice of an animal. Within the context of Allah's complete revelation in the Holy Bible, we see that Allah offers the only Way not to just *cover* but to completely and eternally *remove* our sin and shame.

The Fifth Result of Sin

> GENESIS 3:22-24
> *And the Lord God (Allah) said, "The man has now become like one of us, knowing good and evil. He must not be allowed to reach out his hand and take also from the tree of life and eat, and live forever." So the Lord God banished him from the Garden of Eden to work the ground from which he had been taken. After he drove the man out, he placed on the east side of the*

Garden of Eden cherubim and a flaming sword flashing back and forth to guard the way to the tree of life.

The fifth result of sin mentioned here is humankind's broken relationship with holy Allah and our expulsion from Paradise.

Questions

- How many sins did Adam and Hawa commit in order to cause these horrible results?
- How many good deeds did Allah say they can do to return?
- Why did Allah provide Adam and Hawa with adequate covering even though He was about to expel them from Paradise?

Allah reveals throughout the Holy Bible that He is most merciful and most forgiving. Then why did Allah not simply forgive them to avoid pain and death outside of Paradise for His beloved creation?

Please pause here and ponder what you've read.

- Explain the passages in your own words as if you were sharing it with someone else.
- Explain how the passages make you think or feel and why.
- What do the passages tell you about Allah?
- What do the passages tell you about you and your relationship with Allah?
- What action do you think Allah wants from you according to these passages?
- As a result, create an "I will . . ." statement to obey Allah according to these passages.

Chapter Conclusion

When I first read Genesis chapter three, I found it extremely heavy, with the consequences of sin being much more destructive and deadly than I originally thought. Sin brings deep and immense shame and tremendous loss: loss of purity, loss of intimacy with Allah, loss of Paradise, loss of life. A holy Allah demands and deserves absolute obedience. These verses prompted many difficult questions in my own heart. As I studied, I saw the following truths come to light:

1. It only took one sin for humanity to be expelled from Paradise with Allah. Our own sins sever our connection to Allah and block us from Paradise.
2. There was nothing Adam and Hawa could do to get back into Paradise. Allah reveals throughout the Holy Bible that good deeds are not adequate to return to Paradise. Thankfully, Allah does reveal His One and only Way for restoring us into an everlasting and perfect relationship with Him in Paradise.
3. Allah provides for us. Even though you and I are not in Paradise, Allah reveals throughout the Holy Bible that He cares for us and our needs. Allah has provided what we need from the start. Allah is both holy and loving. The world changed with sin, but Allah's love and provision never change!
4. Allah reveals throughout the Holy Bible that holiness and righteousness demand a complete and perfect restoration. Forgiveness and mercy are not adequate for humankind restoration with Allah in Paradise. The good news is that Allah does provide the One and only holy, righteous, and complete Way, and He does reveal it in the Holy Bible.

In the next chapter we will read about a new character Allah introduces in the Holy Bible: Ibrahim (Abraham in English). Allah then reveals through Ibrahim the first of Allah's progressive revelations to guide you and me to the One and only Way you and I can be restored to Paradise to live forever with Him.

Will you pray that Allah will reveal the truth to you about His Word?

- What specific requests do you have for Allah now?
- If you have a Christian friend, then ask him or her to pray with you in the name of Jesus.
- If you do not know or have access to a Christian near you, then please contact us with your specific prayer request (pray@WordofAllah.org).

Be specific with any need or issue that Allah can do for you today, even if it is miraculous. It does not mean that Allah will perform a physical miracle for you. The greatest miracle Allah desires for you is eternal life in Paradise, and He has already accomplished that. In this book we study how you can have this greatest miracle from Allah. It is already yours if you choose it.

Jesus Forgives

LUKE 7:36–50

When one of the Pharisees invited Jesus to have dinner with him, he went to the Pharisee's house and reclined at the table. A woman in that town who lived a sinful life learned that Jesus was eating at the Pharisee's house, so she came there with an alabaster jar of perfume. As she stood behind him at his feet weeping, she began to wet his feet with her tears. Then she wiped them with her hair, kissed them and poured perfume on them.

When the Pharisee who invited him saw this, he said to himself, "If this man were a prophet, he would know who is touching him and what kind of woman she is—that she is a sinner." Jesus answered him, "Simon, I have something to tell you."

"Tell me, teacher," he said.

"Two people owed money to a certain moneylender. One owed him five hundred denarii, and the other fifty. Neither of them had the money to pay him back, so he forgave the debts of both. Now which of them will love him more?"

Simon replied, "I suppose the one who had the bigger debt forgiven."

"You have judged correctly," Jesus said.

The he turned toward the woman and said to Simon, "Do you see this woman? I came into your house. You did not give me any water for my feet, but she wet my feet with her tears and wiped them with her hair. You did not give me a kiss, but this woman, from the time I entered, has not stopped kissing my feet. You did not put oil on my head, but she has poured perfume on my feet. Therefore, I tell you, her many sins have been forgiven—as her great love has shown. But whoever has been forgiven little loves little."

Then Jesus said to her, "Your sins are forgiven." "The other guests began to say among themselves, "Who is this who even forgives sins?"

Jesus said to the woman, "Your faith has saved you; go in peace."

Women Help Jesus

LUKE 8:1-3

After this, Jesus traveled about from one town and village to another, proclaiming the good news of the kingdom of God (Allah). The twelve were with him, and also some women who had been cured of evil spirits and diseases: Mary (called Magdalene) from whom seven demons had come out; Joanna the wife of Chuza, the manager of Herod's household; Susanna; and many others. These women were helping to support them out of their own means.

Jesus Forgave Me

As I shared with you earlier, more than twenty years ago I did not believe in Allah, or Jesus. I was guilty of many sins. I was guilty of most of the things in Galatians 5:19-21:

The acts of the flesh are obvious: sexual immorality, impurity and debauchery, idolatry and witchcraft; hatred, discord, jealousy, fits of rage, selfish ambition, dissensions, factions, and envy; drunkenness, orgies, and the like ....

Despite all my sin, Allah never stopped desiring that I know and accept His truth. He desires the same for you. After a journey of study, prayer, and discovery, I accepted and believed the truth. Allah's Holy Spirit filled my heart. Little by little, Allah transformed me. He cleansed me of my shame, just as He desires to do for every human being.

Allah desires for us to live, filled with His Spirit with joy, peace, forbearance, kindness, goodness, faithfulness, gentleness and self-control according to Galatians 5:22-23.

My prayer is that you will know, believe, and accept the truth and will experience the fruit of Allah's Holy Spirit.

Prayer for Allah's Forgiveness

PSALM 51:1–17

Have mercy on me, O God (Allah), according to your unfailing love; according to your great compassion blot out my transgressions.

Wash away all my iniquity and cleanse me from my sin.

For I know my transgressions, and my sin is always before me.

Against you, you only, have I sinned and done what is evil in your sight; so you are right in your verdict and justified when you judge.

Surely I was sinful at birth, sinful from the time my mother conceived me.

Yet you desired faithfulness even in the womb; you taught me wisdom in that secret place.

Cleanse me with hyssop, and I will be clean; wash me, and I will be whiter than snow.

Let me hear joy and gladness; let the bones you have crushed rejoice.

Hide your face from my sins and blot out all my iniquity.

Create in me a pure heart, O God (Allah), and renew a steadfast spirit within me.

Do not cast me out from your presence or take your Holy Spirit from me.

Restore to me the joy of your salvation and grant me a willing spirit, to sustain me.

Then I will teach transgressors your ways, so that sinners will turn back to you.

Deliver me from the guilt of bloodshed, O God (Allah), you who are God my Savior, and my tongue will sing of your righteousness.

Open my lips, Lord, and my mouth will declare your praise.

You do not delight in sacrifice, or I would bring it; you do not take pleasure in burnt offerings.

My sacrifice, O God (Allah), is a broken spirit; a broken and contrite heart you, God (Allah), will not despise.

Chapter Six

Ibrahim and Sacrifice

As always, let us begin with a prayer:

We pray that the Holy Spirit of Allah will fill us to reveal, guide, and teach us the truth as we discover Allah's Word and revelations in the Holy Bible. In Jesus's name, amen!

As a child, I felt like I had a loving relationship with Allah. As an adult, aware of my sin and the shame it caused me, I stopped seeking Allah and did not want a relationship with Him. But now, looking back, I see that Allah repeatedly took the initiative to restore my relationship with Him. As we saw in the previous chapter, after the first human sinned, Allah still lovingly initiated doing what was necessary to restore the relationship.

This chapter introduces the first of Allah's progressive revelations over a period of 1,500 years to guide you and me to the One and only Way you and I can be restored into relationship with Allah—an eternity with Him in Paradise. I'm excited to take this next step of the study with you.

Allah's First Sacrifice

We'll start by reviewing the state of Adam and Hawa's condition when they chose to disobey Allah—and what Allah's response to that sin was.

GENESIS 3:21-24

The Lord God made garments of skin for Adam and his wife and clothed them. And the Lord God said, "The man has now become like one of us, knowing good and evil. He must not be allowed to reach out his hand and take also from the tree of life and eat, and live forever." So the Lord God banished him from the Garden of Eden to work the ground from which he had been taken. After he drove the man out, he placed on the east side of the Garden of Eden cherubim and a flaming sword flashing back and forth to guard the way to the tree of life.

When Adam and Hawa sinned, Allah made clothing of animal skin to cover their nakedness and shame. This literal and symbolic covering required the first death because their clothing demanded the sacrifice of life—in this case, an animal.

As we continue through the story in Genesis 4, Allah reveals how sacrifice points to the One and only Way to be restored into an eternity with Him in Paradise.

Humankind's First Recorded Sacrifice

GENESIS 4:1-5

Adam made love to his wife Eve (Hawa), and she became pregnant and gave birth to Cain (Qabil). She said, "With the help of the Lord I have brought forth a man." Later she gave birth to his brother Abel (Habil). Now Abel (Habil) kept flocks, and Cain (Qabil) worked the soil. In the course of time Cain (Qabil) brought some of the fruits of the soil as an offering to the Lord. And Abel (Habil) also brought an offering—fat portions from some of the firstborn of his flock. The Lord looked with favor on Abel (Habil) and his offering, but on Cain (Qabil) and his offering he did not look with favor. So Cain (Qabil) was very angry, and his face was downcast.

Please pause here and ponder what you've read.

- Explain the passages in your own words as if you were sharing them with someone else.
- Explain how the passages make you think or feel and why.
- What do the passages tell you about Allah?
- What do the passages tell you about you and your relationship with Allah?
- What action do you think Allah wants from you according to these passages?
- As a result, create an "I will..." statement to obey Allah according to these passages.

Additional Questions

- What did Habil offer that Allah looked upon with favor?
- How did Habil learn to offer the firstborn of his flock as sacrifice?

In Genesis 3:21, Allah made the first sacrifice by killing an animal to create coverings for Adam and Hawa. Many years had passed between Genesis 3:21 and 4:1–5; Habil had been born and was old enough to keep flocks at this point in the story. In the years between Genesis 3 and Genesis 4, Allah must have instructed humankind about offering a firstborn of the flock as sacrifice.

Throughout the Holy Bible, Allah reveals how and why sacrifice is an essential part of His One and only Way for humankind to be restored to Paradise with Him. In this book, we will study together some of the main revelations that point us to Allah's Way.

With that in mind, we're going to move ahead a few chapters in the story of Genesis. (Otherwise, this book would be significantly longer!) I encourage you to feel free, however, to read the passages of the Holy Bible that we don't discuss in this book; in fact, I wholeheartedly urge you to read the entire Holy Bible. It is worth it! Allah transforms lives on earth (Allah did with me!) and for eternity of the people who know and believe His Word. That begins when we read it.

As a brief transition to where we are going next, I want to point out a few important points along the way. In Genesis 12, Allah introduces the story of Abraham (Ibrahim in Arabic) and reveals His saving plan for humankind through his descendants. In Genesis 15:6, speaking of Ibrahim, we read, *"And he believed the Lord, and he counted it to him as righteousness."*

Approximately 2,000 years pass between Genesis 4 and 12. Much of the human history can be summarized in the chapters by noting what has been typical of humankind throughout history: People repeatedly and quickly strayed away from the One and true Allah. But Ibrahim believed Allah.

Before we move into the next portion of this study, please read Genesis 22.

Now, let us look at Genesis 22 a few verses at a time so we can better comprehend Allah's revelation.

Allah's Demand of Sacrifice from Ibrahim

GENESIS 22:1–8

Some time later God (Allah) tested Abraham (Ibrahim). He said to him, "Abraham (Ibrahim)!"

"Here I am," he replied.

Then God (Allah) said, "Take your son, your only son, whom you love—Isaac—and go to the region of Moriah. Sacrifice him there as a burnt offering on a mountain I will show you."

Early in the next morning Abraham (Ibrahim) got up and loaded his donkey. He took with him two of his servants and his son Isaac. When he had cut enough wood for the burnt offering, he set out for the place God (Allah) had told him about. On the third day, Abraham (Ibrahim) looked up and saw the place in the distance. He said to his servants, "Stay here with the donkey while I and the boy go over there. We will worship and then we will come back to you."

Abraham (Ibrahim) took the wood for the burnt offering and placed it on his son Isaac, and he himself carried the fire and the knife. As the two of them went on together, Isaac spoke up and said to his father Abraham, "Father?"

"Yes, my son?" Abraham (Ibrahim) replied.

"The fire and wood are here," Isaac said, "but where is the lamb for the burnt offering?"

Abraham (Ibrahim) answered, "God (Allah) himself will provide the lamb for the burnt offering, my son." And the two of them went on together.

Please pause here and ponder what you've read.

- Explain the passage in your own words as if you were sharing it with someone else.
- Explain how the passage makes you think or feel and why.
- What does the passage tell you about Allah?
- What does the passage tell you about you and your relationship with Allah?
- What action do you think Allah wants from you according to this passage?
- As a result, create an "I will . . ." statement to obey Allah according to this passage.

Additional Question

- What do you think Ibrahim was thinking in offering his son as a sacrifice?

I mentioned earlier that Allah helps us understand the revelations in His Word from within His Word. I found the answer to the question above in Hebrews 11.

HEBREWS 11:17-19

By faith Abraham (Ibrahim), when God (Allah) tested him, offered Isaac as a sacrifice. He who had embraced the promises was about to sacrifice his one and only son, even though God (Allah) had said to him, "It is through Isaac that your offspring will be reckoned." Abraham (Ibrahim) reasoned that God (Allah) could even raise the dead, and so in a manner of speaking he did receive Isaac back from death.

Substitutionary Sacrifice

GENESIS 22:9-14

When they reached the place God (Allah) had told him about, Abraham (Ibrahim) built an altar there and arranged the wood on it. He bound his son Isaac and laid him on the altar, on top of the wood. Then he reached out his hand and took the knife to slay his son. But the angel of the Lord called out to him from heaven, "Abraham (Ibrahim)! Abraham (Ibrahim)!"

"Here I am," he replied.

"Do not lay a hand on the boy," he said. "Do not do anything to him. Now I know that you fear God (Allah), because you have not withheld from me your son, your only son." Abraham (Ibrahim) looked up and there in a thicket he saw a ram caught by its horns. He went over and took the ram and sacrificed it as a burnt offering instead of his son. So Abraham (Ibrahim) called that place The Lord Will Provide. And to this day it is said, "On the mountain of the Lord it will be provided."

All Nations Will Be Blessed

GENESIS 22:15-18

The angel of the Lord called to Abraham (Ibrahim) from heaven a second time and said, "I swear by myself, declares the Lord, that because you have done this and have not withheld your son, your only son, I will surely bless you and make your descendants as numerous as the stars in the sky and as the sand on the seashore. Your descendants will take possession of the cities of their enemies, and through your offspring all nations on earth will be blessed, because you have obeyed me."

Please pause here and ponder what you've read.

- Explain the passages in your own words as if you were sharing it with someone else.
- Explain how the passages make you think or feel and why.
- What do the passages tell you about Allah?
- What do the passages tell you about you and your relationship with Allah?
- What action do you think Allah wants from you according to these passages?
- As a result, create an "I will . . ." statement to obey Allah according to these passages.

Chapter Conclusion

When I first read these stories in the Holy Scriptures, I did not understand certain things, and I had many questions. I wondered:

- *Why did Allah sacrifice things, and expect humans to also do the same?*
- *Why did Allah demand a sacrifice of the firstborn of the flock?*
- *Is it okay with Allah that I have such questions?*
- *Does Allah reveal answers to such questions?*

I felt spiritually hungry. I needed answers to these questions and so many others. The more I read of Allah's Word throughout the Holy Bible, the more I understood that Allah welcomes and answers our questions!

You and I have only read a little of Allah's Word in the Holy Bible and already He has revealed that He is holy, righteous, complete, and perfect. As we continue to study Allah's Word throughout the Holy Bible, we will see that His plan to restore humankind to eternal Paradise with Him must also be holy, righteous, complete, and perfect.

Will you pray that Allah will reveal the truth to you about His Word?

- What specific requests do you have for Allah now?
- If you have a Christian friend, then ask him or her to pray with you in the name of Jesus.
- If you do not know or have access to a Christian near you, then please contact us with your specific prayer request (pray@wordofAllah.org).

Be specific with any need or issue that Allah can do for you today, even if it is miraculous. It does not mean that Allah will perform a physical miracle for you. The greatest miracle Allah desires for you is eternal life in Paradise, and He has already accomplished that. In this book we study how you can have this greatest miracle from Allah. It is already yours if you choose it.

A Friend of Jesus Dies

JOHN 11:1-16

Now a man named Lazarus was sick. He was from Bethany, the village of Mary and her sister Martha. (This Mary, whose brother Lazarus now lay sick, was the same one who poured perfume on the Lord and wiped his feet with her hair.) So the sisters sent word to Jesus, "Lord, the one you love is sick."

When he heard this, Jesus said, "This sickness will not end in death. No, it is for God's glory so that God's Son may be glorified through it." Now Jesus loved Martha and her sister and Lazarus. So when he heard that Lazarus was sick, he stayed where he was two more days, and then he said to his disciples, "Let us go back to Judea."

"But Rabbi," they said, "a short while ago the Jews there tried to stone you, and yet you are going back?" Jesus answered, "Are there not twelve hours of daylight? Anyone who walks in the daytime will not stumble, for they see by the world's light. It is when a person walks at night that they stumble, for they have no light."

After he had said this, he went on to tell them, "Our friend Lazarus has fallen asleep; but I am going there to wake him up." His disciples replied, "Lord, if he sleeps, he will get better." Jesus had been speaking of his death, but his disciples thought he meant natural sleep.

So then he told them plainly, "Lazarus is dead, and for your sake I am glad I was not there, so that you may believe. But let us go to him." Then Thomas (also known as Didymus) said to the rest of the disciples, "Let us also go, that we may die with him."

Jesus Is the Resurrection and Life

JOHN 11:17–37

On his arrival, Jesus found that Lazarus had already been in the tomb for four days. Now Bethany was less than two miles from Jerusalem, and many Jews had come to Martha and Mary to comfort them in the loss of their brother. When Martha heard that Jesus was coming, she went out to meet him, but Mary stayed at home.

"Lord," Martha said to Jesus, "if you had been here, my brother would not have died. But I know that even God (Allah) will give you whatever you ask." Jesus said to her, "Your brother will rise again." Martha answered, "I know he will rise again in the resurrection at the last day."

Jesus said to her, "I am the resurrection and the life. The one who believes in me will live, even though they die; and whoever lives by believing in me will never die. Do you believe this?" "Yes, Lord," she replied, "I believe that you are the Messiah (Al Masih), the Son of God (Allah), who is to come into the world."

After she had said this, she went back and called her sister Mary aside. "The Teacher is here," she said, "and is asking for you." When Mary heard this, she got up quickly and went to him. Now Jesus had not yet entered the village, but was still at the place where Martha had met him. When the Jews who had been with Mary in the house, comforting her, noticed how quickly she got up and went out, they followed her, supposing she was going to the tomb to mourn there.

When Mary reached the place where Jesus was and saw him, she fell at his feet and said, "Lord, if you had been here, my brother would not have died." When Jesus saw her weeping, and the Jews who had come along with her also weeping, he was deeply moved in spirit and troubled. "Where have you laid him?" he asked. "Come and see, Lord," they replied.

Jesus wept.

Then the Jews said, "See how he loved him!" But some of them said, "Could not he who opened the eyes of the blind man have kept this man from dying?"

Jesus Raises the Dead

JOHN 11:38–44

Jesus, once more deeply moved, came to the tomb. It was a cave with a stone laid across the entrance. "Take away the stone," he *said. "But, Lord," said Martha, the sister of the dead man, "by this time there is a bad odor, for he has been there four days."*

Then Jesus said, "Did I not tell you that if you believe, you will see the glory of God (Allah)?" So they took away the stone. Then Jesus looked up and said, "Father, I thank you that you have heard me. I knew that you always hear me, but I said this for the benefit of the people standing here, that they may believe that you sent me."

When he had said this, Jesus called in a loud voice, "Lazarus, come out!" The dead man came out, his hands and feet wrapped with strips of linen, and a cloth around his face. Jesus said to them, "Take off the grave clothes and let him go."

How Allah Saved My Life—Part Two

In chapter three of this book, I shared about the first time I contemplated suicide, and how Jesus saved me. My struggles with my health, finances, and life in general, however, continued for the next few years. At the time, I was in my mid-forties, and life seemed to only get worse. Before long, my health and physical state worsened and once again, my family was back in a financial crisis.

I had reached the breaking point. I was no longer just *contemplating* ending my life; I was completely determined to do so. I had, however, learned about the trauma a family suffers when one of its members commits suicide. Not wanting to harm my family's emotional well-being, I planned multiple ways to end my life in such a way that it would look like an accident. Obviously, my attempts failed, thanks be to Allah.

One of the ways I planned to end my life "accidentally" was through my illness of diabetes. As a diabetic, if I take too much diabetic medication, my blood sugar level can drop too low, causing my death. So I planned to overdose on my medicine, but make it appear that I simply accidentally miscalculated how much medication I took.

I told my family that I was going on a personal retreat to an isolated place. I rented and prepaid for a place to stay, ensuring that no one would come bother me. I knew that eventually, though, the owners would come to check on me, only to find my dead body.

That week, however, regardless of what I did or how much diabetic medication I took, my blood sugar level remained constant. My body acted as if I did not have diabetes. I was very angry with Allah, as it appeared to me that He was not allowing me to end my life. I cried out to Him, pleading my case to allow me to die then. Eventually, Allah spoke to me. It was in still whispers in my mind, yet Allah's voice was clear to me.

I heard Allah say to me: "I am Allah. You are not! Obey my voice! Stop now with your foolishness. Just trust and obey! Get up and leave this place!"

I did. How could I not?

Allah miraculously intervened and stopped my diabetes for a week, but Allah did not heal me permanently from diabetes. Immediately after Allah saved me from suicide, my diabetic condition returned. If I took too much diabetic medicine, my blood sugar level dropped dangerously low. If I consumed too much carbohydrates or sugars, my blood sugar levels increased to dangerous highs.

For the next five years after Allah saved my life, I prayed consistently, in the name of Jesus, that He would miraculously heal me permanently from diabetes. Allah did not. In all that time, I never got a response from Allah about my health at all—whether He would heal my diabetes or not.

Then one day while I was checking my blood sugar level, I heard that same still voice in my head that I heard five years prior: "How many times per day do you do that?"

I said: "Three to seven times per day."

He said: "At this time, I will not heal you from diabetes. Instead, every day when you check your blood sugar, let it be a memorial so that you will remember how and why I saved your life."

I knelt, wept, and praised Allah.

The physical miracle Allah did with me was to save my life. Then, in His love, Allah gave me the gift to not physically heal me from diabetes, but through it to allow me three to seven times per day to remember that He saved me miraculously.

The biggest and eternal miracle is that Allah saved me spiritually. He calmed the storms of my life and transformed my heart. As of the writing of this book, I'm alive in my late fifties, living a life of trusting and obeying Allah. I believe that one of the purposes Allah saved me for was to serve Him through iHOPE Ministries and to write this book to you.

My prayer is that Allah will lead you into the truth through His Word, saving you spiritually as He did with me.

Insha'Allah.

Allah's Love and Protection

PSALM 36

I have a message from God (Allah) in my heart concerning the sinfulness of the wicked: There is no fear of God (Allah) before their eyes.

In their own eyes they flatter themselves too much to detect or hate their sin.

The words of their mouths are wicked and deceitful; they fail to act wisely or do good.

Even on their beds they plot evil; they commit themselves to a sinful course and do not reject what is wrong.

Your love, Lord, reaches to the heavens, your faithfulness to the skies.

Your righteousness is like the highest mountains, your justice like the great deep. You, Lord, preserve both people and animals.

How priceless is your unfailing love, O God (Allah)! People take refuge in the shadow of your wings.

They feast on the abundance of your house; you give them drink from your river of delights.

For with you is the fountain of life; in your light we see light.

Continue your love to those who know you, your righteousness to the upright in heart.

May the foot of the proud not come against me, nor the hand of the wicked drive me away.

See how the evildoers lie fallen—thrown down, not able to rise!

Chapter Seven

Musa, Israel, and Sacrifice

As always, let us begin with a prayer:

We pray that the Holy Spirit of Allah will fill us to reveal, guide, and teach us the truth as we discover Allah's Word and revelations in the Holy Bible. In Jesus's name, amen!

As you can see from the little I shared of my story in previous chapters, Allah always spoke clearly to me at key points in my life to guide me in His will and path.

In this chapter, we will review a little more of Allah's progressive revelation to guide humankind, you and me, to the One and only Way we can be restored into an eternity with Allah in Paradise. We will see Allah speak plainly and clearly to Musa, to the ancient nation of Israel, and to Egypt. Allah clearly revealed His will to all of them. In the Holy Bible, Allah continues to communicate His revelation to each human.

Our study in this chapter comes from the book of Exodus in the Holy Bible. From Genesis 23 to where we'll start in Exodus 3, about 400 years pass. (As always, please feel free to pause and read the stories Allah reveals in those chapters.) During that time, Ibrahim's grandson Jacob (Yaqub in Arabic) and his family moved to Egypt. Allah changed Jacob's name to Israel. Joseph (Yusuf in Arabic), one of Israel's sons, became a great ruler in Egypt. Meanwhile, as has happened repeatedly throughout history, their descendants strayed away from the One and only true Allah. Eventually, Israel's descendants became slaves in Egypt. As their living conditions worsened, they began to cry out to Allah for help.

In response, Allah called Musa to lead the people of Israel out of slavery in Egypt.

EXODUS 3:13-15

Moses (Musa) said to God (Allah), "Suppose I go to the Israelites and say to them, 'The God of your fathers has sent me to you' and they ask me, 'What is his name?' Then what shall I tell them?"

God (Allah) said to Moses (Musa), "I AM WHO I AM. This is what you are to say to the Israelites: 'I AM has sent me to you.'" God also said to Moses (Musa), "Say to the Israelites, 'The Lord, the God of your fathers—the God of Abraham (Ibrahim), the God of Isaac and the God of Jacob (Yaqub)—has sent me to you. This is my name forever, the name you shall call me from generation to generation.'"

Allah's Message to Israel

EXODUS 6:6-7

"Therefore, say to the Israelites: 'I am the Lord, and I will bring you out from under the yoke of the Egyptians. I will free you from being slaves to them, and I will redeem you with an outstretched arm and with mighty acts of judgment. I will take you

as my own people, and I will be your God. Then you will know that I am the Lord your God, who brought you out from under the yoke of the Egyptians."

Through Musa, Allah points the people of Israel to Himself so they will once again know the One and only true Allah. Allah announces that He will do mighty acts of judgment against Egypt.

Allah's Message to Egypt

EXODUS 5:1-2

Afterward Moses (Musa) and Aaron (Harun in Arabic) went to Pharaoh and said, "This is what the Lord, the God of Israel, says: 'Let my people go, so that they may hold a festival to me in the wilderness.'" Pharaoh said, "Who is the Lord, that I should obey him and let Israel go? I do not know the Lord and I will not let Israel go."

EXODUS 7:4-5

". . . Then I will lay my hand on Egypt and with mighty acts of judgment I will bring out my divisions, my people the Israelites. And the Egyptians will know that I am the Lord when I stretch out my hand against Egypt and bring the Israelites out of it."

Pharaoh, the Egyptian leader, and his people, like the rest of the people of the world, had strayed away from and did not know the One and only true Allah. They worshiped animals, nature, and human-made things. He shows Himself as the One and only true Allah to the unrepentant Egypt through ten mighty acts of judgment: the ten plagues. They are described in Exodus 7:14 through Exodus 12:32. Notice the theme of the ultimate sovereignty of Allah throughout these chapters as you read the following verses:

EXODUS 7:17

This is what the Lord says: By this you will know that I am the Lord...

EXODUS 8:10

"... so that you may know there is no one like the Lord our God."

EXODUS 8:22

"... so that you will know that I, the Lord, am in this land."

EXODUS 9:13–14, 29

Then the Lord said to Moses (Musa), "Get up early in the morning, confront Pharaoh and say to him, 'This is what the Lord, the God of the Hebrews, says: ... so you may know that there is no one like me in all the earth ... so you may know that the earth is the Lord's.'"

EXODUS 10:2

"... that you may know that I am the Lord."

EXODUS 12:12

"... I will bring judgment on all the gods of Egypt. I am the Lord."

Please pause here and ponder what you've read.

- Explain the passages in your own words as if you were sharing it with someone else.
- Explain how the passages make you think or feel and why.
- What do the passages tell you about Allah?
- What do the passages tell you about you and your relationship with Allah?
- What action do you think Allah wants from you according to these passages?

- As a result, create an "I will..." statement to obey Allah according to these passages.

Allah's Sacrifice Demand from Musa and Israel

Please read all of Exodus 12.

Throughout each of the ten plagues to which Allah subjects the Egyptians, the people of Israel were still slaves in Egypt. With the last plague, Allah reveals a little bit more about the significance of the substitutionary blood sacrifice and why He consistently requires it.

Let's look at some of the verses you just read and examine them for revelations from Allah.

Lamb without Defect

EXODUS 12:1-6

The Lord said to Moses (Musa) and Aaron (Harun) in Egypt, "This month is to be for you the first month, the first month of your year. Tell the whole community of Israel that on the tenth day of this month each man is to take a lamb for his family, one for each household.

"If any household is too small for a whole lamb, they must share one with their nearest neighbor, having taken into account the number of people there are. You are to determine the amount of lamb needed in accordance with what each person will eat. The animals you choose must be year-old males without defect, and you may take them from the sheep or the goats. Take care of them until the fourteenth day of the month, when all

the members of the community of Israel must slaughter them at twilight."

The Blood of the Sacrifice

EXODUS 12:7

"Then they are to take some of the blood and put it on the sides and tops of the doorframes of the houses where they eat the lambs."

The Passover

EXODUS 12:12-13

"On that same night I will pass through Egypt and strike down every firstborn of both people and animals, and I will bring judgment on all the gods of Egypt. I am the Lord. The blood will be a sign for you on the houses where you are, and when I see the blood, I will pass over you. No destructive plague will touch you when I strike Egypt."

EXODUS 12:21-30

Then Moses (Musa) summoned all the elders of Israel and said to them, "Go at once and select the animals for your families and slaughter the Passover lamb. Take a bunch of hyssop, dip it into the blood in the basin and put some of the blood on the top and on both sides of the doorframe.

"None of you shall go out of the door of your house until morning. When the Lord goes through the land to strike down the Egyptians, he will see the blood on the top and sides of the doorframe and will pass over that doorway, and he will not permit the destroyer to enter your houses and strike you down.

Obey these instructions as a lasting ordinance for you and your descendants. When you enter the land that the Lord will give you as he promised, observe this ceremony.

"And when your children ask you, 'What does this ceremony mean to you?' then tell them, 'It is the Passover sacrifice to the Lord, who passed over the houses of the Israelites in Egypt and spared our homes when he struck down the Egyptians.'" Then the people bowed down and worshiped. The Israelites did just what the Lord commanded Moses (Musa) and Aaron (Harun).

At midnight the Lord struck down all the firstborn in Egypt, from the firstborn of Pharaoh, who sat on the throne, to the firstborn of the prisoner, who was in the dungeon, and the firstborn of all the livestock as well. Pharaoh and all his officials and all the Egyptians got up during the night, and there was loud wailing in Egypt, for there was not a house without someone dead.

Please pause here and ponder what you've read.

- Explain the passages in your own words as if you were sharing it with someone else.
- Explain how the passages make you think or feel and why.
- What do the passages tell you about Allah?
- What do the passages tell you about you and your relationship with Allah?
- What action do you think Allah wants from you according to these passages?
- As a result, create an "I will . . ." statement to obey Allah according to these passages.

In chapter five of this book, we read about the first recorded animal blood sacrifice made by a human. The offering was by Habil (Abel in English) in Genesis 4:4. In Exodus 12, Allah reveals a little more than He did before about the need for a blood sacrifice. The blood of the lamb without defect was a sign so that Allah's judgment passed over the people under its protection. Only the people who accepted the blood of the sacrifice were saved from Allah's righteous judgment.

Chapter Conclusion

When I first read these Holy Scriptures, I did not yet understand their full context or their vital implications for my life. It was only after I finished reading all of Allah's revelations in the Holy Bible that I comprehended that my eternal destination, whether Paradise or hell, depended on what I understood, believed, and did regarding His truth.

I finally understood that just as the people of Israel had to be saved by Allah from Egypt, I had to be saved by Allah from hell. Just as the firstborn of the people of Israel had to be saved from Allah's righteous judgment of death by the sacrificial blood of a perfect lamb, I too needed to be saved from Allah's righteous judgment of hell by the sacrifice that He Himself provides.

Since Allah is holy, righteous, complete and perfect, His plan to save you and me and restore us to Paradise must also reflect His character and attributes. As we continue to study Allah's Word in the Holy Bible, you will see that He reveals His plan just as clearly as He revealed Himself to Musa, the Israelites, and the Egyptians.

Will you pray that Allah will reveal the truth to you about His Word?

- What specific requests do you have for Allah now?
- If you have a Christian friend, then ask him or her to pray with you in the name of Jesus.

- If you do not know or have access to a Christian near you, then please contact us with your specific prayer request (pray@wordofAllah.org).

Be specific with any need or issue that Allah can do for you today, even if it is miraculous. It does not mean that Allah will perform a physical miracle for you. The greatest miracle Allah desires for you is eternal life in Paradise, and He has already accomplished that. In this book we study how you can have this greatest miracle from Allah. It is already yours if you choose it.

Jesus Feeds Thousands with Two Fish

MATTHEW 14:13-19

When Jesus heard what had happened, he withdrew by boat privately to a solitary place. Hearing of this, the crowds followed him on foot from the towns. When Jesus landed and saw a large crowd, he had compassion on them and healed their sick. As evening approached, the disciples came to him and said, "This is a remote place, and it's already getting late. Send the crowds away, so they can go to the villages and buy themselves some food.

Jesus replied, "They do not need to go away. You give them something to eat."

"We have here only five loaves of bread and two fish," they answered.

"Bring them here to me," he said. And he directed the people to sit down on the grass. Taking the five loaves and the two fish and looking up to heaven, he gave thanks and broke the loaves. Then he gave them to the disciples, and the disciples gave them

to the people. They all ate and were satisfied, and the disciples picked up twelve basketfuls of broken pieces that were left over. The number of those who ate was about five thousand men, besides women and children.

Walking on Deep Sea Water

MATTHEW 14:22-33

Immediately Jesus made the disciples get into the boat and go on ahead of him to the other side, while he dismissed the crowd. After he had dismissed them, he went up on a mountainside by himself to pray. Later that night, he was there alone, and the boat was already a considerable distance from land, buffeted by the waves because the wind was against it.

Shortly before dawn Jesus went out to them, walking on the lake. When the disciples saw him walking on the lake, they were terrified. "It's a ghost," they said, and cried out in fear.

But Jesus immediately said to them: "Take courage! It is I. Don't be afraid."

"Lord, if it's you," Peter replied, "tell me to come to you on the water."

"Come," he said.

Then Peter got down out of the boat, walked on the water and came toward Jesus. But when he saw the wind, he was afraid and, beginning to sink, cried out, "Lord, save me!"

Immediately Jesus reached out his hand and caught him. "You of little faith," he said, "why did you doubt?"

And when they climbed into the boat, the wind died down. Then those who were in the boat worshiped him, saying, "Truly you are the Son of God."

Jesus Heals the Sick

MATTHEW 14:34-36

When they had crossed over, they landed at Gennesaret. And when the men of that place recognized Jesus, they sent word to all the surrounding country. People brought all their sick to him and begged him to let the sick just touch the edge of his cloak, and all who touched it were healed.

How Allah Provided for My Family Financially

After the Holy Spirit of Allah transformed my heart and replaced the anger and hate I once felt toward Muslims with the love of Jesus, I sensed Allah calling me to quit my job and be in full-time ministry. I was afraid; my faith was still weak when it came to trusting for Allah's financial provision. Karen, my wife, encouraged me strongly to listen to Allah's calling, quit my job, and to serve Him. For me, full-time ministry meant sharing with Muslims what Allah did with me, the study of His Word in the Holy Bible, centered around His Way to restore us to Paradise with Him.

I struggled with Allah's call to ministry. I am knowledgeable enough, and I study a lot on my own, but I do not have college or religious seminary education. I had a good consulting job in 2010, and Karen had a better job than me, but we were still in a big financial hole. By March 2011, the sense Karen and I had was getting stronger every day that I was to quit my job and go into full-time ministry.

So we looked at our budget and financial picture if I were to quit my job and lose my income. Even after we did every possible cut in our budget, we would still be short around $15,000 per year. We simply could not do it financially. So, for the next month, we fasted and prayed (in the name of Jesus), asking Allah to give us wisdom and guide us. I boldly asked that Allah confirm that we were hearing his calling correctly with a sign, showing us that he would provide the finances we needed.

After one month of fasting and praying in the name of Jesus, we did not hear anything from Allah, nor did we have an affirming sign. So we broke the fast. I concluded that we did not sense Allah's calling correctly, and that I was not yet to quit my job.

The very next morning, a former work colleague of Karen called her to see if she would be interested in a position with the company he was working for at the time. After several interviews the next week, they offered Karen a job that would increase her net pay by $18,000 per year. Karen already had strong financial faith, encouraging me all along to just trust Allah and obey his call immediately.

My financial faith was weak. Most gracious, loving, and kind Allah knew all that. Allah forgave my weak faith and gave me the faith-strengthening sign I needed to move forward. Allah reminded me of the stories of various people throughout the Holy Bible that had weak faith like I used to have, and how at times Allah also gave them faith-strengthening signs.

Allah has already provided eternal provision for you and me for everyone that comes to Him through his One and only Way. May the Holy Spirit of Allah help you see that Way through our study together. Insha'Allah!

Allah Is the Greatest

PSALM 145

I will exalt you, my God the King; I will praise your name for ever and ever.

Every day I will praise you and extol your name for ever and ever.

Great is the Lord and most worthy of praise; his greatness no one can fathom.

One generation commends your works to another; they tell of your mighty acts.

They speak of the glorious splendor of your majesty—and I will meditate on your wonderful works.

They tell of the power of your awesome works—and I will proclaim your great deeds.

They celebrate your abundant goodness and joyfully sing of your righteousness.

The Lord is gracious and compassionate, slow to anger and rich in love.

The Lord is good to all; he has compassion on all he has made.

All your works praise you, Lord; your faithful people extol you.

They tell of the glory of your kingdom and speak of your might, so that all the people may know of your mighty acts and the glorious splendor of your kingdom.

Your kingdom is an everlasting kingdom, and your dominion endures through all generations. The Lord is trustworthy in all he promises and faithful in all he does.

The Lord upholds all who fall and lifts up all who are bowed down.

The eyes of all look to you, and you give them their food at the proper time.

You open your hand and satisfy the desires of every living thing.

The Lord is righteous in all his ways and faithful in all he does.

The Lord is near to all who call on him, to all who call on him in truth.

He fulfills the desires of those who fear him; he hears their cry and saves them.

The Lord watches over all who love him, but all the wicked he will destroy.

My mouth will speak in praise of the Lord. Let every creature praise his holy name for ever and ever.

Chapter Eight

Allah's Requirement

As always, let us begin with a prayer:

We pray that the Holy Spirit of Allah will fill us to reveal, guide, and teach us the truth as we discover Allah's Word and revelations in the Holy Bible. In Jesus's name, amen!

In the previous chapter we studied how Allah saved Ibrahim's descendants out of slavery, just as He promised Ibrahim hundreds of years before. Ibrahim's descendants could not earn their way out of slavery. They needed Allah to initiate saving them, and to provide the way to set them free.

As I've shared with you in previous chapters, I lived as a slave to sin for several decades. I needed Allah to initiate saving me and to provide the way to set me free. Allah did!

In this chapter we will study what Allah requires as necessary for the One and only Way you and I can be set free from slavery to sin and brought into an eternity with Allah in Paradise, and why Allah requires it.

Legal Requirement or Death!

> EXODUS 13:1-2
>
> *The Lord said to Moses (Musa), "Consecrate to me every firstborn male. The first offspring of every womb among the Israelites belongs to me, whether human or animal."*

Within the Word of Allah in the Holy Bible, consecrate means to make holy by giving or dedicating to Allah.

> EXODUS 13:12-16
>
> *"... you are to give over to the Lord the first offspring of every womb. All the firstborn males of your livestock belong to the Lord. Redeem with a lamb every firstborn donkey, but if you do not redeem it, break its neck. Redeem every firstborn among your sons. In days to come, when your son asks you, 'What does this mean?' say to him, 'With a mighty hand the Lord brought us out of Egypt, out of the land of slavery.'*
>
> *"'When Pharaoh stubbornly refused to let us go, the Lord killed the firstborn of both people and animals in Egypt. This is why I sacrifice to the Lord the first male offspring of every womb and redeem each of my firstborn sons.' And it will be like a sign on your hand and a symbol on your forehead that the Lord brought us out of Egypt with his mighty hand."*

To redeem means "to gain or regain possession of something in exchange for payments." Redeem also means legal "compensation to clear a debt." In these verses, Allah is reminding humans that because humankind sinned, death is their destination or debt. For a human to live, Allah requires that compensation be made. In the scriptures above, we see that at this point in history, for a firstborn child to live, the legal compensation was the sacrifice of an unblemished lamb.

Allah's command here serves as a constant reminder to the Israelites that without the sacrifice of the unblemished lamb, every firstborn in Egypt died in the tenth plague.

Just as He has been doing since humankind sinned, Allah is revealing that there must be a substitutionary sacrifice to legally clear the debt of the human soul from death. Allah warned humankind in Paradise before humans sinned that sin brings death into the world. Knowing when He created us that humans would fall into the trap of sin, Allah, in His loving, holy, just, and righteous character, had a complete and holy plan to save the human soul. In these holy Scriptures, Allah is continuing His progressive revelation to reveal this plan, the One and only Way your soul and mine can be redeemed from hell.

In the next passages of holy Scriptures, Allah reveals other commands and lessons relevant to our topic. Please turn to the next section of the Holy Bible: Leviticus.

Sacrifices for Sin

In Leviticus 4 and 5, Allah gives detailed instructions regarding His commandments about ongoing blood sacrifices of animals for the legal compensation required for the forgiveness of sin for the people. All the animals had to be without blemish or defect. He commands in Leviticus 4:4, 4:15, and 4:24 that the animals be killed, and He explains the reason why the animals were to be slaughtered. Let's look at a few verses together:

LEVITICUS 4:26

"In this way the priest will make atonement for the leader's sin, and he will be forgiven."

LEVITICUS 4:31

"... make atonement for them, and they will be forgiven."

LEVITICUS 4:35 AND 5:10 REPEAT THE SAME WORDS:

"... will make atonement for them for the sin they have committed, and they will be forgiven."

LEVITICUS 5:6

"... make atonement for them for their sin."

LEVITICUS 5:13

"... make atonement for them for any of these sins they have committed, and they will be forgiven."

And then, in Leviticus 17:11, Allah reveals why blood sacrifices were necessary:

"For the life of a creature is in the blood, and I have given it to you to make atonement for yourselves on the altar; it is the blood that makes atonement for one's life."

Atonement means "making amends for a wrong one has done." We will now begin to study Allah's revelations about what and how things were to be done. Everything had to be done exactly as Allah commanded.

Unholy Human with a Holy Allah

LEVITICUS 10:1–3

Aaron's (Harun's) sons Nadab and Abihu took their censers, put fire in them, and added incense; and they offered unauthorized fire before the Lord, contrary to his command. So fire came out from the presence of the Lord and consumed them, and they died before the Lord. Moses (Musa) then said to Aaron (Harun), "This is what the Lord spoke of when he said: 'Among those who *approach me I will be proved holy; in the sight of all the people I will be honored."' Aaron (Harun) remained silent.*

Question
- Why did Allah kill two priests bringing him an offering?

Harun was the first high priest of Allah's people. Two of Harun's sons, priests as well, brought an offering to Allah. But the offering, the persons offering it, and the way they presented it to Allah were not as He instructed. So Allah judged and killed them immediately. Allah's instructions were clear. These two priests were neither ignorant nor misinformed; they knew what Allah commanded, and they chose to do things their way.

In these verses, Allah teaches the painful lesson that humans are unholy, and cannot survive the presence of holy Allah. Just as darkness cannot coexist with light, unholy cannot survive the presence of what is holy. The only way humans can survive being with Allah is by following His strict and detailed instructions for the provision He says is needed.

Please pause here and ponder what you've read.
- Explain the passages in your own words as if you were sharing it with someone else.
- Explain how the passages make you think or feel and why.
- What do the passages tell you about Allah?
- What do the passages tell you about you and your relationship with Allah?
- What action do you think Allah wants from you according to these passages?
- As a result, create an "I will . . ." statement to obey Allah according to these passages.

"Most Holy Place"

Before we move into the next part of our study, please read Leviticus 16 in its entirety.

Now, let us look at Leviticus 16 more closely so we can understand Allah's revelations here. This is another deep study. It will require a patient and deliberate process. After all, we are finite created beings, seeking to understand what our infinite Creator is revealing to us through the Holy Bible. Go slowly and carefully through these verses because they will help you in your own journey to discover Allah's One and only Way to be saved from eternal hell.

LEVITICUS 16:1-2

The Lord spoke to Moses (Musa) after the death of the two sons of Aaron (Harun) who died when they approached the Lord. The Lord said to Moses: "Tell your brother Aaron that he is not to come whenever he chooses into the Most Holy Place behind the curtain in front of the atonement cover on the ark, or else he will die. For I will appear in the cloud over the atonement cover."

In the chapters between Exodus 13 and Leviticus 16, Allah has revealed many detailed and strict instructions regarding the requirements for a human to survive in the presence of holy Allah. As instructed by Allah, the people built a place that was called the "tent of meeting." This was where Allah met with His people.

Within the tent of meeting, Allah's divine presence filled an area that is mentioned in the verses above: the "Most Holy Place behind the curtain." No one was allowed to enter into the divine presence of Allah in the Most Holy Place except the high priest. Here in Leviticus 16, Harun was the high priest. If anyone else tried to enter the Most Holy Place, he would die, just as Harun's two sons had.

We also see in these verses that the High Priest could not "come whenever he chooses into the Most Holy Place." Even he could only enter Allah's divine presence once a year, on the Day of Atonement, which is the reference of Leviticus 16.

Amends for Sin

As the one chosen to enter the Most Holy Place to make the atoning sacrifices before Allah on behalf of the people, the high priest (Harun in this case) had to do so in a very specific way. Let's continue our reading . . .

LEVITICUS 16:3-5

"This is how Aaron (Harun) is to enter the Most Holy Place: He must first bring a young bull for a sin offering and a ram for a burnt offering. He is to put on the sacred linen tunic, with linen undergarments next to his body; he is to tie the linen sash around him and put on the linen turban. These are sacred garments; so he must bathe himself with water before he puts them on. From the Israelite community he is to take two male goats for a sin offering and a ram for a burnt offering."

Amends for the High Priest

LEVITICUS 16:6-7

"Aaron (Harun) is to offer the bull for his own sin offering to make atonement for himself and his household. Then he is to take the two goats and present them before the Lord at the entrance to the tent of meeting."

As a human, even the high priest was not considered clean or free from sin. He had to select a bull for a sin sacrifice to make atonement (amends) with Allah for himself and his household, before he could be the mediator between Allah and the rest of the people.

Amends for the People

LEVITICUS 16:7–10

"Then he is to take the two goats and present them before the Lord at the entrance to the tent of meeting. He is to cast lots for the two goats—one lot for the Lord and the other for the scapegoat. Aaron (Harun) shall bring the goat whose lot falls to the Lord and sacrifice it for a sin offering. But the goat chosen by lot as the scapegoat shall be presented alive before the Lord to be used for making atonement by sending it into the wilderness as a scapegoat."

Goats were selected for the sin offering for the rest of the people. Everyone sins and needs forgiveness.

Complete Cleansing to Enter the "Most Holy Place"

LEVITICUS 16:11–12

"Aaron (Harun) shall bring the bull for his own sin offering to make atonement for himself and his household, and he is to slaughter the bull for his own sin offering. He is to take a censer full of burning coals from the altar before the Lord and two handfuls of finely ground fragrant incense and take them behind the curtain."

LEVITICUS 16:13–14

"He is to put the incense on the fire before the Lord, and the smoke of the incense will conceal the atonement cover above the tablets of the covenant law, so that he will not die. He is to take some of the bull's blood and with his finger sprinkle it on the front of the atonement cover; then he shall sprinkle some of it with his finger seven times before the atonement cover."

The First Goat

LEVITICUS 16:15-16
"He shall then slaughter the goat for the sin offering for the people and take its blood behind the curtain and do with it as he did with the bull's blood: He shall sprinkle it on the atonement cover and in front of it. In this way he will make atonement for the Most Holy Place because of the uncleanness and rebellion of the Israelites, whatever their sins have been. He is to do the same for the tent of meeting, which is among them in the midst of their uncleanness."

All these rituals were symbolic in nature. The symbolical atonement was required even for the "Most Holy Place because of the uncleanness and rebellion" of the people. Allah does not yet reveal what these rituals symbolize until later in the Holy Bible, which we will study subsequently in this book.

Only the High Priest Can Open the Way

LEVITICUS 16:17
"No one is to be in the tent of meeting from the time Aaron (Harun) goes in to make atonement in the Most Holy Place until he comes out, having made atonement for himself, his household and the whole community of Israel."

Within Allah's revelation of the Holy Bible, the "tent of meeting" typifies heaven because it is where Allah is. Only the high priest, and only when and how instructed by Allah, may approach Allah's dwelling place. If the high priest does not do it correctly, he will die. By following Allah's specific commands and directions, the high priest could safely enter Allah's presence and offer amends, or an atoning sacrifice, on behalf of the people.

Completion of the Ceremony

LEVITICUS 16:18–22

"Then he shall come out to the altar that is before the Lord and make atonement for it. He shall take some of the bull's blood and some of the goat's blood and put it on all the horns of the altar. He shall sprinkle some of the blood on it with his finger seven times to cleanse it and to consecrate it from the uncleanness of the Israelites.

When Aaron (Harun) has finished making atonement for the Most Holy Place, the tent of meeting and the altar, he shall bring forward the live goat. He is to lay both hands on the head of the live goat and confess over it all the wickedness and rebellion of the Israelites—all their sins—and put them on the goat's head. He shall send the goat away into the wilderness in the care of someone appointed for the task. The goat will carry on itself all their sins to a remote place; and the man shall release it in the wilderness.

In the first part of the Atonement ceremony, the blood sacrifices of firstborn animals without defect (as instructed earlier in the Holy Bible by Allah), atoned (made amends) for the sins of the priests and the rest of the people. Now the sins were symbolically removed from the atoned-for people and transferred to the goat, which was taken into the wilderness away from the people.

To summarize the verses we've just reviewed together, we see that Allah commanded the people of Israel to observe the annual Day of Atonement. This detailed, religious ceremony included external cleansing, symbolically pointing to the internal cleansing of the human heart, mind, and soul. The Day of Atonement also included substitutionary blood sacrifices that symbolically and formally represented the forgiveness of and removal of sin from the people of Allah. Only then did the people safely enter Allah's presence without dying.

Now that we have studied most of Leviticus 16 together, please pause and think about what you have read and respond to the questions below.

- Explain the passages in your own words as if you were sharing it with someone else.
- Explain how the passages make you think or feel and why.
- What do the passages tell you about Allah?
- What do the passages tell you about you and your relationship with Allah?
- What action do you think Allah wants from you according to these passages?
- As a result, create an "I will . . ." statement to obey Allah according to these passages.

Chapter Conclusion

When I first read passages in the Holy Bible, such as those in Leviticus 16, I wondered why Allah required substitutionary blood sacrifices. Blood sacrifices are not something we see in our modern times, so they may not make sense to you either. But we see that up to this point in Allah's revelations in the Holy Bible, He was clear that without the blood of a substitutionary sacrifice that is without defect there is no atonement for sin, nor restoration of humankind (you and me) to Allah's Holy Presence.

Allah gave hundreds of other commandments related to cleansing and sacrifices, like those we have read here in Leviticus 16. Allah revealed that part of the purposes of these rules and ceremonies was to serve as a constant reminder of our need for cleansing and atonement. Allah eventually reveals that these ceremonial laws and rituals, including the animal blood sacrifices, did not take away our sins. Like the clothing He made for Adam and Hawa, the sacrifices simply covered sin temporarily. But all these things point us to Allah's One and only Way that can take away our sins, atone us, redeem us, cleanse us, purify us, and allow us to live in Paradise with Allah forever.

Allah is the infinite, all-knowing, all-powerful Creator. You and I are very tiny, finite, created beings. In His infinite love, wisdom, mercy, and patience, Allah progressively revealed and communicated His plan at a pace and in a way that makes it possible for you and me to process and grasp.

Allah, throughout the Holy Bible, reveals that He is holy, righteous, complete, and perfect. Allah reveals that His plan to bring you and me, humankind, back to Paradise with Him forever, must also be holy, righteous, complete, and perfect. Forgiveness and mercy, two of Allah's attributes, do not by themselves form a holy, righteous, complete, and perfect plan. And Allah's plan is most wonderful!

I am so excited to continue this vital journey of discovering Allah's Word together with you so we will know Allah's holy, righteous, complete, perfect, One and only Way that you and I can be restored to eternal Paradise with Allah.

Will you pray that Allah will reveal the truth to you about His Word?

- What specific requests do you have for Allah now?
- If you have a Christian friend, then ask him or her to pray with you in the name of Jesus.

- If you do not know or have access to a Christian near you, then please contact us with your specific prayer request (pray@wordofAllah.org).

Be specific with any need or issue that Allah can do for you today, even if it is miraculous. It does not mean that Allah will perform a physical miracle for you. The greatest miracle Allah desires for you is eternal life in Paradise, and He has already accomplished that. In this book we study how you can have this greatest miracle from Allah. It is already yours if you choose it.

Jesus Teaches: Love Your Enemies

LUKE 6:27–36

"But to you who are listening I say: Love your enemies, do good to those who hate you, bless those who curse you, pray for those who mistreat you. If someone slaps you on one cheek, turn to them the other also. If someone takes your coat, do not withhold your shirt from them. Give to everyone who asks you, and if anyone takes what belongs to you, do not demand it back. Do to others as you would have them do to you.

"If you love those who love you, what credit is that to you? Even sinners love those who love them. And if you do good to those who are good to you, what credit is that to you? Even sinners do that. And if you lend to those from whom you expect repayment, what credit is that to you? Even sinners lend to sinners, expecting to be repaid in full. But love your enemies, do good to them, and lend to them without expecting to get anything back. Then your reward will be great, and you will be children of the Most High, because he is kind to the ungrateful and wicked. Be merciful, just as your Father is merciful."

Jesus Heals a Servant

LUKE 7:1–10

When Jesus had finished saying all this to the people who were listening, he entered Capernaum. There a centurion's servant, whom his master valued highly, was sick and about to die. The centurion heard of Jesus and sent some elders of the Jews to him, asking him to come and heal his servant. When they came to Jesus, they pleaded earnestly with him, "This man deserves to have you do this, because he loves our nation and has built our synagogue." So Jesus went with them.

He was not far from the house when the centurion sent friends to say to him: "Lord, don't trouble yourself, for I do not deserve to have you come under my roof. That is why I did not even consider myself worthy to come to you. But say the word, and my servant will be healed. For I myself am a man under authority, with soldiers under me. I tell this one, 'Go,' and he goes; and that one, 'Come,' and he comes. I say to my servant, 'Do this,' and he does it."

When Jesus heard this, he was amazed at him, and turning to the crowd following him, he said, "I tell you, I have not found such great faith even in Israel." Then the men who had been sent returned to the house and found the servant well.

Jesus Raises a Widow's Son

LUKE 7:11–17

Soon afterward, Jesus went to a town called Nain, and his disciples and a large crowd went along with him. As he approached the town gate, a dead person was being carried out—the only son of his mother, and she was a widow. And a large crowd *from the town was with her. When the Lord saw her, his heart went out to her and he said, "Don't cry."*

Then he went up and touched the bier they were carrying him on, and the bearers stood still. He said, "Young man, I say to you, get up!" The dead man sat up and began to talk, and Jesus gave him back to his mother.

They were all filled with awe and praised God (Allah). "A great prophet has appeared among us," they said. "God (Allah) has come to help his people." This news about Jesus spread throughout Judea and the surrounding country.

Jesus Heals Mohammad

A Muslim family in the Middle East had a son, "Mohammad." Even as a child, Mohammad always seemed sad, very shy, and did not join other boys for fun and games. Mohammad was intelligent and had excellent grades in school. When he was eight years old, Mohammad began to try to hurt himself. Doctors believed Mohammad was under the dark influence of demons and suggested his parents take him to the imam for special prayers.

Mohammad's parents began increasing their daily prayers at the masjid (mosque) up to twelve times per day. Prominent imams in their country prayed over Mohammad. They put Quranic verses throughout their house and things belonging to Mohammad. They did this for the next ten years, but Mohammad was not healed.

As a teenager, Mohammad began contemplating suicide as a way to escape his worsening feelings of sadness and hopelessness. Doctors then diagnosed him with chronic depression and put him on special medications, because even though at times Mohammad felt better, the depression never went away. Despite all these challenges,

Mohammad did well in school. When he was old enough, his parents brought him to America in 2014 to attend a university.

One day during lunch, Mohammad, as usual, sat alone to eat. An American student, "Paul," could see that Mohammad looked sad and asked him what was wrong. Mohammad could not explain why he decided to open up to a stranger, but he confided in Paul and told him all about his struggles since childhood. Paul told him that he was a "follower of Jesus" and offered to pray for him "in the name of Jesus." Mohammad explained to Paul all about the prayers everyone had tried for over ten years, but nothing worked.

But Mohammad thought, "Why not?" and accepted Paul's offer. Paul put his hands on Mohammad's shoulders, bowed his head, closed his eyes, and began to pray "in the name of Jesus." In that moment, Mohammad felt warmth throughout his body. He later explained to Paul that it felt in that moment as if spiritual hands had opened him up, taken out his depressed soul, and replaced it with a healthy one.

Instantly, Mohammad experienced feelings he had never felt before in his life. He felt happier than he had ever felt, deep in his soul. He could not stop smiling, which turned to laughter. Then he began leaping with deep joy. That special day in 2014, Mohammad was healed from his lifelong condition of chronic depression. He immediately stopped taking any medications and has not needed them ever since then.

Mohammad believes Allah healed him because of Jesus.

May Allah provide the healing you need, in the name of Jesus, amen!

Six Passages about Healing

PSALM 30:10-12

Hear, Lord, and be merciful to me; Lord, be my help.

You turned my wailing into dancing; you removed my sackcloth and clothed me with joy,

That my heart may sing your praises and not be silent. Lord my God, I will praise you forever.

PSALM 73:26

My flesh and my heart may fail, but God (Allah) is the strength of my heart and my portion forever.

PSALM 103:2-5

Praise the Lord, my soul, and forget not all his benefits—

Who forgives all your sins and heals all your diseases,

Who redeems your life from the pit and crowns you with love and compassion,

Who satisfies your desires with good things so that your youth is renewed like the eagle's.

JAMES 5:14

Is anyone among you sick? Let them call the elders of the church to pray over them and anoint them with oil in the name of the Lord.

MATTHEW 11:28-30, JESUS INVITES YOU . . .

"Come to me, all you who are weary and burdened, and I will give you rest. Take my yoke upon you and learn from me, for I am gentle and humble in heart, and you will find rest for your souls. For my yoke is easy and my burden is light."

Chapter Nine

Allah's Law

As always, let us begin with a prayer:
We pray that the Holy Spirit of Allah will fill us to reveal, guide, and teach us the truth as we discover Allah's Word and revelations in the Holy Bible. In Jesus's name, amen!

Now that we have an understanding of the sacrifices Allah required to cover, make amends, or atone for sin, let's turn back a few pages in the Holy Bible to look at Allah's Law—the standards by which He judges sin. For our study this time, we will start in Exodus 19.

As always, I encourage you to feel free to read the stories in the passages that we have skipped over. They are exciting and I'm sure you don't want to miss them! Here's a very brief summary of what happens between Exodus 13–19: Allah miraculously, with visible signs and wonders, led the people of Israel out of slavery in Egypt. Allah defeated those who tried to prevent the Israelites from leaving, and He miraculously provided everything the people needed to survive the nearly two-month journey (approximately 380 kilometers) before their first major stop: Sinai.

Allah's First Holy Nation

EXODUS 19:1-6

On the first day of the third month after the Israelites left Egypt—on that very day—they came to the Desert of Sinai. After they set out from Rephidim, they entered the Desert of Sinai, and Israel camped there in the desert in front of the mountain.

Then Moses (Musa) went up to God (Allah), and the Lord called to him from the mountain and said, "This is what you are to say to the descendants of Jacob (Yaqub) and what you are to tell the people of Israel: 'You yourselves have seen what I did to Egypt, and how I carried you on eagles' wings and brought you to myself. Now if you obey me fully and keep my covenant, then out of all nations you will be my treasured possession. Although the whole earth is mine, you will be for me a kingdom of priests and a holy nation.' These are the words you are to speak to the Israelites."

Questions

- What kind of kingdom did Allah call ancient Israel to be?
- What kind of nation did Allah call ancient Israel to be?

In establishing the ancient people of Israel as a nation, Allah kept a promise He repeated to Ibrahim, and to Ibrahim's offspring. Let's reread the promise that Allah gave to Ibrahim:

GENESIS 22:17-18

"I will surely bless you and make your descendants as numerous as the stars in the sky and as the sand on the seashore. Your descendants will take possession of the cities of their enemies, and through your offspring all nations on earth will be blessed, because you have obeyed me."

Question

- What did Allah promise He would do through Ibrahim's *descendants* to "all nations on earth"?

Throughout history, people had repeatedly and quickly strayed away from the One and only true Allah (and continue to do so today). Throughout the Holy Bible, we read numerous accounts of Allah bringing mighty acts of judgment on those who chose not to follow Him, including the ten plagues He afflicted upon Egypt. We looked at one of Allah's revealed purposes or explanations for this judgment in Exodus 9, verses 14 and 16.

" . . . I will send the full force of my plagues against you and against your officials and your people, so you may know that there is no one like me in all the earth. . . . that I might show you my power and that my name might be proclaimed in all the earth."

In summary, Allah called the ancient nation of Israel (the descendants of Ibrahim) to be His instrument to bless the whole world by pointing all to the One and only true Allah. As such, this nation needed to be holy. Their sins needed to be covered to remain in relationship with Allah. To guide and govern this new nation, Allah gave ancient Israel, through Musa, His Law.

The summary of Allah's perfect Law to govern an imperfect people is found in The Ten Commandments in Exodus 20, which will be the launching point for our study in the remainder of this session. I believe that every human can benefit from knowing and applying to their lives these ten commandments. In my own life, I saw my relationship with Allah and with other humans improve on every level once I learned and began to apply His Law to my personal life. Let's study them now.

Allah's Ten Commandments

EXODUS 20:1-2

And God (Allah) spoke all these words: "I am the Lord your God, who brought you out of Egypt, out of the land of slavery."

COMMANDMENT #1—EXODUS 20:3

"You shall have no other gods before me."

COMMANDMENT #2—EXODUS 20:4-6

"You shall not make for yourself an image in the form of anything in heaven above or on the earth beneath or in the waters below. You shall not bow down to them or worship them; for I, the Lord your God, am a jealous God, punishing the children for the sin of the parents to the third and fourth generation of those who hate me, but showing love to a thousand generations of those who love me and keep my commandments."

COMMANDMENT #3—EXODUS 20:7

"You shall not misuse the name of the Lord your God, for the Lord will not hold anyone guiltless who misuses his name."

COMMANDMENT #4—EXODUS 20:8-11

"Remember the Sabbath day by keeping it holy. Six days you shall labor and do all your work, but the seventh day is a sabbath to the Lord your God. On it you shall not do any work, neither you, nor your son or daughter, nor your male or female servant, nor your animals, nor any foreigner residing in your towns. For in six days the Lord made the heavens and the earth, the sea, and all that is in them, but he rested on the seventh day. Therefore the Lord blessed the Sabbath day and made it holy."

Please pause here and ponder what you've read.

- Explain the passages in your own words as if you were sharing it with someone else.
- Explain how the passages make you think or feel and why.
- What do the passages tell you about Allah?
- What do the passages tell you about you and your relationship with Allah?
- What action do you think Allah wants from you according to these passages?
- As a result, create an "I will . . ." statement to obey Allah according to these passages.

Summary of the Commandments 1–4

Around twenty years prior to writing this book, I began to read and study Allah's revelations in the Holy Bible. As I continued to seek infinite Allah daily, He helped tiny, finite me gain a deeper understanding of the rich meaning and purpose behind each of the Ten Commandments. Allah promises in His Word that He will do the same for you.

The best way for you to understand how these laws apply to your daily life is to study them for yourself throughout the Holy Bible. Through that process, Allah will transform your life, as He did mine. For now, I believe it may be helpful to you for me to share a summary of what Allah teaches about the first four commandments in the Holy Bible.

In Deuteronomy 6:4–5, Allah reveals who He is: "... *The Lord our God, the Lord is one. Love the Lord your God with all your heart and with all your soul and with all your strength.*"

The first four commandments are about our relationship with Allah, which is the most important part of a human's life. When we have the right relationship with the One and only true Allah, then everything else that is good can follow. Allah's Law commands us to put Him first in our lives. We are not to worship anything or anyone other than Him. We must treat His name with respect and reverence, and we must be intentional about remembering Him.

COMMANDMENT #5—EXODUS 20:12

"Honor your father and your mother, so that you may live long in the land the Lord your God is giving you."

COMMANDMENT #6—EXODUS 20:13

"You shall not murder."

COMMANDMENT #7—EXODUS 20:14

"You shall not commit adultery."

COMMANDMENT #8—EXODUS 20:15

"You shall not steal."

COMMANDMENT #9—EXODUS 20:16

"You shall not give false testimony against your neighbor."

COMMANDMENT #10—EXODUS 20:17

"You shall not covet your neighbor's house. You shall not covet your neighbor's wife, or his male or female servant, his ox or donkey, or anything that belongs to your neighbor."

Please pause here and ponder what you've read.

- Explain the passages in your own words as if you were sharing it with someone else.
- Explain how the passages make you feel and why.
- What do the passages tell you about Allah?

- What do the passages tell you about you and your relationship with Allah?
- What action do you think Allah wants from you according to these passages?
- As a result, create an "I will..." statement to obey Allah according to these passages.

Summary of Commandments 5–10

As He does with other parts of Scripture, Allah reveals His purpose and meaning through the Holy Bible. In Leviticus 19:18 we can see a summary of these six commandments:

"... *love your neighbor as yourself. I am the Lord.*"

The last six commandments concern our relationship with others. Allah's commandments bless the lives of every human that obeys them and make them a blessing to others. In my own life, I saw my relationship with other humans improve on every level once I learned and began to apply His Law to my personal life.

Allah's Revelations of The Ten Commandments

Later in the Holy Bible, Allah summarizes The Ten Commandments through Jesus in Matthew 22:37–40: "... *Love the Lord your God with all your heart and with all your soul and with all your mind. This is the first and greatest commandment. And the second is like it: Love your neighbor as yourself. All the Law and the Prophets hang on these two commandments.*"

Jesus is referred to as Isa ibn Maryam in the Quran, and also called Isa al-Masih by some of my Muslim friends. Approximately 1,400 years passed from when Musa lived to the time of Jesus's life.

Throughout its history as revealed by Allah in the Holy Bible, the ancient nation of Israel, neither the people nor their priests, ever obeyed Allah's Law as required by Him. As I continued reading Allah's Word, I realized I am also guilty of the same. Even when I try to live rightly before Allah, I still sin. No one can uphold Allah's Law perfectly.

Throughout the Holy Bible, Allah progressively revealed the meaning and intended application of His Law. In this next section, we will review what Allah says about these commandments.

Allah's Expected Application of Commandment #6

MATTHEW 5:21–24

"You have heard that it was said to the people long ago, 'You shall not murder, and anyone who murders will be subject to judgment.' But I tell you that anyone who is angry with a brother or sister will be subject to judgment. Again, anyone who says to a brother or sister, 'Raca,' is answerable to the court. And anyone who says, 'You fool!' will be in danger of the fire of hell."

"Therefore, if you are offering your gift at the altar and there remember that your brother or sister has something against you, leave your gift there in front of the altar. First go and be reconciled to them; then come and offer your gift."

Raca is an Aramaic word that can be translated into English as *empty; empty one; foolish; worthless*. Within the context of the whole of Allah's revelations throughout the Holy Bible, anger, *Raca* or "You fool!" toward another human being (a being who is created in the image of Allah) is murder in the heart and mind. These words are applied in connection with hate, disrespect, and abuse (verbal, emotional, etc.) of another human being. Allah reveals that murder is not merely a physical action, but it begins and can be done in the heart, mind, and soul. Hate-filled words are forms of spiritual murders that occur in the inner being of a person, in the heart, mind, and soul. Hate is the opposite of Allah's attribute of love. Remember what we read from 1 John 4:8: Allah *is* love.

In my life, with hateful thoughts and words, I have murdered others in my heart, mind, and spirit. As much as I try to avoid such thoughts, anger and fear still bring them to mind from time to time even now. I know now that the hate I once felt toward Muslims is viewed by Allah as murder. I am so thankful that through Jesus, Allah has transformed my heart and filled it with His love for Muslims.

Question

- How do you murder other human beings in your heart, mind, and spirit?

It is when we love others as ourselves that we fulfill Allah's last six commandments. As we do that, we reflect our fulfillment of Allah's first four commandments to love Allah with all our hearts, souls, and minds.

Allah's Expected Application of Commandment #7

MATTHEW 5:27-28

"You have heard that it was said, 'You shall not commit adultery.' But I tell you that anyone who looks at a woman lustfully has already committed adultery with her in his heart."

In my life, I have committed adultery in my mind and heart. Impure thoughts, unfortunately, still periodically cross my mind. Allah views an impure sexual thought as sin.

> **Question**
>
> - Have you lusted in your mind or heart for another human being that you are not married to?

Allah's Other Definitions of His Commandments

1 CORINTHIANS 6:9-10

Or do you not know that wrongdoers will not inherit the kingdom of God (Allah)? Do not be deceived: Neither the sexually immoral nor idolaters nor adulterers nor men who have sex with men nor thieves nor greedy nor drunkards nor slanderers nor swindlers will inherit the kingdom of God (Allah).

In my life, I have committed the sin of greed in my heart and mind. I also mistakenly, and at times innocently, inaccurately misrepresented something about someone else that damaged their reputation (this is the meaning of slander). And unfortunately, periodically I still do these things.

> **Question**
>
> - Do you recognize any of the sins listed in the verses above as your own?

GALATIANS 5:19-21

The acts of the flesh are obvious: sexual immorality, impurity and debauchery; idolatry and witchcraft; hatred, discord, jealousy, fits of rage, selfish ambition, dissension, factions and envy; drunkenness, orgies, and the like. I warn you, as I did before, that those who live like this will not inherit the kingdom of God (Allah).

In my life, in addition to the things I have already confessed to earlier, I have also committed the sins of "discord, jealousy, fits of rage, selfish ambition, dissension, factions and envy." And unfortunately, periodically I still do these things.

Question

- Do you recognize any of the sins listed in the verses above as your own?

EPHESIANS 5:3–5

But among you there must not be even a hint of sexual immorality, or of any kind of impurity, or of greed, because these are improper for God's holy people. Nor should there be obscenity, foolish talk or coarse joking, which are out of place, but rather thanksgiving. For of this you can be sure: No immoral, impure or greedy person—such a person is an idolater—has any inheritance in the kingdom of Christ (Al-Masih) and of God (Allah).

Unfortunately, periodically I still commit the sins of flipping someone else off in anger, or using obscene language to someone else, or saying such things in my mind and heart. These are the life-application definitions of obscenity and foolish talk.

Question

- Do you recognize any of the sins listed in the verses above as your own?

COLOSSIANS 3:5–8

Put to death, therefore, whatever belongs to your earthly nature: sexual immorality, impurity, lust, evil desires and greed, which is idolatry. Because of these, the wrath of God (Allah) is coming. You used to walk in these ways, in the life you once lived. But now you must also rid yourselves of all such things as these: anger, rage, malice, slander, and filthy language from your lips.

Allah reveals through these verses that a person who does these things is an idolater. An idolater is defined as someone who worships idols, which would be disobedience to Allah's first four commandments dealing with our relationship with Him. But Allah reveals that desiring or being greedy for something or someone, more than Allah, is idolatry. To me, this is one of the most difficult things to be consciously aware of whether I am desiring anything or anyone more than Allah. Allah's standards are perfect and holy. I find it impossible for a human to live perfectly holy according to Allah's standards.

JAMES 2:8-9

If you really keep the royal law found in Scripture, "Love your neighbor as yourself," you are doing right. But if you show favoritism, you sin and are convicted by the law as lawbreakers.

Unfortunately, periodically I still commit the sin of favoritism, therefore convicted as breaking Allah's Law. For example, at an event, I would try to sit next to someone who is more influential, powerful, or wealthier than someone else. How about you?

JAMES 2:10-11

For whoever keeps the whole law and yet stumbles at just one point is guilty of breaking all of it. For he who said, "You shall not commit adultery," also said, 'You shall not murder." If you do not commit adultery but do commit murder, you have become a lawbreaker.

Please pause here and ponder what you've read.

- Explain the passages in your own words as if you were sharing it with someone else.
- Explain how the passages make you think or feel and why.
- What do the passages tell you about Allah?
- What do the passages tell you about you and your relationship with Allah?
- What action do you think Allah wants from you according to these passages?
- As a result, create an "I will . . ." statement to obey Allah according to these passages.

All have sinned!

Allah makes it abundantly clear throughout the Holy Bible that "All have sinned!" Please read four examples of what Allah reveals about this in His Word:

1 KINGS 8:46

"... for there is no one that does not commit sin ..."

ECCLESIASTES 7:20

Indeed, there is no one on earth who is righteous, no one who does what is right and never sins.

ROMANS 3:23

... for all have sinned and fall short of the glory of God (Allah) ...

1 JOHN 1:8

"*If we claim to be without sin, we deceive ourselves and the truth is not in us.*"

In Allah's holy, righteous, perfect and complete ways and standards, "all have sinned" and fall short of His glory and demand for perfection. As Allah revealed in the Holy Scriptures we reviewed in this chapter, you and I sin in our minds, hearts, and souls, toward Allah, and towards other humans.

The Terrible News

As we have seen so far, Allah's definition of sin is strict (more so than I once believed). His response to sin is equally demanding. Allah is infinitely holy and righteous. His Law is perfect, righteous, just, and wholly good. Allah takes His Law seriously, and He demands that we do the same. Allah also judges our thoughts, feelings, and motives, as well as our actions.

Allah knows that all humans sin and fall woefully short of His glory and His requirement of perfection. The price or punishment for sin is steep: Allah tells us in Romans 6:23, "*The wages of sin is death.*" Just as Allah warned Adam and Hawa in Paradise, sin brings shame, suffering, and death into the world. Since the very first sin, humankind has been experiencing this reality.

Humans, you and I cannot survive Allah's Holy Presence without following perfectly the special provisions He gave. Darkness (we) cannot survive the presence of light (Allah).

But...

The Good News from Allah

Allah said, "*For the wages of sin is death, but the gift of God (Allah) is eternal life in...*"

Allah "is love." Out of His love, Allah created humans, so He is our "Father." Allah wants us to have "eternal life" with Him in Paradise. Because of His great love for us, Allah created us and is leading us toward the One and only Way that reopens the door for you and me to return to Paradise. Once we know, understand, and believe in the One and only Way, we can begin that journey back.

Earlier we read Colossians 3:5–8. If we continue reading in Colossians 3:9–10, we'll see that Allah calls us away from sin and toward Him as a new person: *". . . since you have taken off your old self with its practices and have put on the new self, which is being renewed in knowledge in the image of its Creator."*

Once we know, understand, and believe in Allah's One and only Way, then the spiritual transformation described in these verses can begin. This transformation of the heart, mind, and soul is a lifelong process. Allah is renewing me daily, and it is most wonderful.

ISAIAH 64:4–6

Since ancient times no one has heard, no ear has perceived, no eye has seen any God besides you, who acts on behalf of those who wait for him. You come to the help of those who gladly do right, who remember your ways. But when we continued to sin against them, you were angry. How then can we be saved? All of us have become like one who is unclean, and all our righteous acts are like filthy rags; we all shrivel up like a leaf, and like the wind our sins sweep us away.

"All our righteous acts are like filthy rags."
"Our sins sweep us away."
"How then can we be saved?"

In the next chapter, we will learn more about Allah's answer to that last question from the prophet Isaiah.

Will you pray that Allah will reveal the truth to you about His Word?

- What specific requests do you have for Allah now?
- If you have a Christian friend, then ask him or her to pray with you in the name of Jesus.
- If you do not know or have access to a Christian near you, then please contact us with your specific prayer request (pray@WordofAllah.org).

Be specific with any need or issue that Allah can do for you today, even if it is miraculous. It does not mean that Allah will perform a physical miracle for you. The greatest miracle Allah desires for you is eternal life in Paradise, and He has already accomplished that. In this book we study how you can have this greatest miracle from Allah. It is already yours if you choose it.

The Greatest Commandments

MARK 12:28-34

One of the teachers of the law came and heard them debating. Noticing that Jesus had given them a good answer, he asked him, "Of all the commandments, which is the most important?"

"The most important one," answered Jesus, "is this: 'Hear, O Israel: The Lord our God, the Lord is one. Love the Lord your God with all your heart and with all your soul and with all your mind and with all your strength.' The second is this: 'Love your neighbor as yourself.' There is no commandment greater than these."

"Well said, teacher," the man replied. "You are right in saying that God (Allah) is one and there is no other but him. To love him with all your heart, with all your understanding and with

all your strength, and to love your neighbor as yourself is more important than all burnt offerings and sacrifices."

When Jesus saw that he had answered wisely, he said to him, "You are not far from the kingdom of God (Allah)." And from then no one dared ask him any more questions.

Jesus Heals Deaf and Mute

MARK 7:31-37

Then Jesus left the vicinity of Tyre and went through Sidon, down to the Sea of Galilee and into the region of the Decapolis. There some people brought to him a man who was deaf and could hardly talk, and they begged Jesus to place his hand on him.

After he took him aside, away from the crowd, Jesus put his fingers into the man's ears. Then he spit and touched the man's tongue. He looked up to heaven and with a deep sigh said to him, "Ephphatha!" (which means "Be opened!"). At this, the man's ears were opened, his tongue was loosened, and he began to speak plainly.

Jesus commanded them not to tell anyone. But the more he did so, the more they kept talking about it. People were overwhelmed with amazement. "He has done everything well," they said. "He even makes the deaf hear and the mute speak."

Miracle for Muslim Woman

Years ago, Karen my wife and I traveled to the Middle East to share the love of Jesus with Muslims. One day we were having lunch in a restaurant, and at a table close to ours there was a Muslim woman wearing a hijab, sitting and eating alone. We noticed that she looked very sad, her eyes tearing up at times. Karen approached her and introduced us as Christians visiting the area to share the love of Jesus with Muslims.

After we got to know each other a little, "Amirah" told us why she was sad and crying. Amirah, over thirty years old, had been a full-time caretaker of her sick parents ever since she was a teenager. Her parents had just passed away, and Amirah's brother inherited everything, including the money and the house they lived in. Since the parents had passed away, Amirah's brother had been beating her, denying her access to any money, and demanding she move out of the house before his upcoming wedding.

Amirah felt hopeless about her future. She did not have any job skills, other than taking care of her parents and the household. Amirah thought of herself as too unattractive physically and too old to be a desirable wife. Amirah did not believe she had any legal options to get any of the inheritance or to stop her brother from removing her from what had been her home since childhood. We asked Amirah if we could pray for her "in the name of Jesus," and she accepted. We prayed for her situation, and afterward we exchanged contact information.

Months later, after Karen and I returned to America, we called Amirah. We had not talked with her since we were in the Middle East, but we had prayed for her often. As soon as we identified ourselves on the phone, Amirah shouted with joy, "It's a miracle! It's a miracle! Allah answered your prayers in the name of Jesus."

You see, immediately after our encounter and prayer with Amirah, she went home to discover that her brother's behavior had completely changed toward her. He never beat her again, stopped demanding that she move out of the house where she still lives, and gave her a portion of the inheritance. Amirah believed that it was a miraculous intervention from Allah who changed her brother's heart towards her, in response to the prayer in the name of Jesus. No other prayers prior to that worked.

As of the writing of this book, it has been five years since we met Amirah. Since then, we have visited her several times in the Middle East and have kept in contact with her. She still lives in the house she grew up in and enjoys an improving relationship with her now-married brother. With the inheritance money she received, she opened a successful business.

We continue to pray with Amirah in the name of Jesus, and we have studied Allah's revelations in the Holy Bible with her. Amirah knows and believes in Allah's One and only Way for salvation.

Allah's Perfect Law

PSALM 19:7–14

The law of the Lord is perfect, refreshing the soul. The statutes of the Lord are trustworthy, making wise the simple.

The precepts of the Lord are right, giving joy to the heart. The commands of the Lord are radiant, giving light to the eyes.

The fear of the Lord is pure, enduring forever. The decrees of the Lord are firm, and all of them are righteous.

They are more precious than gold, than much pure gold; they are sweeter than honey, than honey from the honeycomb.

By them your servant is warned; in keeping them there is great reward.

But who can discern their own errors? Forgive my hidden faults.

Keep your servant also from willful sins; may they not rule over me. Then I will be blameless, innocent of great transgression.

May these words of my mouth and this meditation of my heart be pleasing in your sight, Lord, my Rock and my Redeemer.

Chapter Ten

Allah's Promised Servant and Savior

As always, let us begin with a prayer:

We pray that the Holy Spirit of Allah will fill us to reveal, guide, and teach us the truth as we discover Allah's Word and revelations in the Holy Bible. In Jesus's name, amen!

Since the beginning of the Holy Bible, immediately after humankind sinned, Allah slowly but surely began revealing His perfect plan to reconcile you and me to Himself and to restore us to Paradise.

Around 2,700 years ago, through the prophet Isaiah, Allah made revelations about the Servant whom He promised was still to come. Allah revealed that the One and only Way you and I can be saved from hell and into heaven is through this promised Servant.

This is another deep study of the Word of infinite Allah, requiring patient and careful study by finite humans like you and me. It is worth it! That is because it has implications for our eternal destination.

Let's begin by turning to and reading from passages from Isaiah 52 and 53 to learn about the Servant that Allah promised to send to our aid.

Introduction to Allah's Servant

ISAIAH 52:13

See, my servant will act wisely; he will be raised and lifted up and highly exalted.

Allah's Servant "will act wisely" and succeeds. As a result, "he will be raised and lifted up and highly exalted." This is remarkable in light of the next verse Allah reveals about His Servant.

Allah's Servant Disfigured

ISAIAH 52:1

Just as there were many who were appalled at him—his appearance was so disfigured beyond that of any human being and his form marred beyond human likeness—

Before Allah's Servant is "raised and lifted up and highly exalted," many will be "appalled at him—his appearance was so disfigured beyond that of any human being and his form marred beyond human likeness." That verse describes the extreme humiliation and suffering Allah's Servant would endure before his exaltation.

Mystery of Allah's Servant

ISAIAH 52:15
... so he will sprinkle many nations, and kings will shut their mouths because of him. For what they were not told, they will see, and what they have not heard, they will understand.

The Mighty Arm of Allah

ISAIAH 53:1
Who has believed our message and to whom has the arm of the Lord been revealed?

Allah's revelation continues to sound strange to humans, with descriptions like the "arm of the Lord." It is hard for humans to understand and believe that Allah's Servant, here revealed as the arm of Allah, can somehow go through extreme humiliation and suffering.

The Servant's Appearance

ISAIAH 53:
"He grew up before him like a tender shoot, and like a root out of dry ground. He had no beauty or majesty to attract us to him, nothing in his appearance that we should desire him.

Allah reveals that his Servant will be physically weak and frail, "like a tender" plant struggling to grow "like a root out of dry ground." Nothing about his physical appearance or surroundings will make him attractive to humans or make them think he is anything but ordinary.

Allah's Suffering Servant

ISAIAH 53:3-4

He was despised and rejected by mankind, a man of suffering, and familiar with pain. Like one from whom people hide their faces he was despised, and we held him in low esteem. Surely he took up our pain and bore our suffering, yet we considered him punished by God (Allah), stricken by him, and afflicted.

Allah begins to reveal why His Servant suffered. In these verses, Allah reveals that His Servant "took up our pain and bore our suffering." Instead of understanding that Allah's Servant was to do this for our sake, "we considered him punished by" Allah. That is why in Isaiah 53:3 we read that humans despised him and held him in low esteem.

ISAIAH 53:5

But he was pierced for our transgressions, he was crushed for our iniquities; the punishment that brought us peace was on him, and by his wounds we are healed.

Questions

- For whose "transgressions" was the Servant "pierced"?
- For whose "iniquities" was the Servant "crushed"?
- How do we obtain "peace"?
- How are we "healed"?

ISAIAH 53:6

We all, like sheep, have gone astray, each of us has turned to our own way; and the Lord has laid on him the iniquity of us all.

All humans, beginning with the first ones, Adam and Hawa, as Allah reveals throughout the Holy Bible, "have sinned and fall short of the glory of" Allah.

Death of Allah's Servant

ISAIAH 53:7-9

He was oppressed and afflicted, yet he did not open his mouth; he was led like a lamb to the slaughter, and as a sheep before its shearers is silent, so he did not open his mouth. By oppression and judgment he was taken away. Yet who of his generation protested? For he was cut off from the land of the living; for the transgression of my people he was punished. He was assigned a grave with the wicked, and with the rich in his death, though he had done no violence, nor was any deceit in his mouth.

Questions

- What happened to Allah's Promised Servant?
- Why did that happen to Allah's Promised Servant?
- What were the sins of Allah's Promised Servant?

After the Death of Allah's Servant

ISAIAH 53:10

Yet it was the Lord's will to crush him and cause him to suffer, and though the Lord makes his life an offering for sin, he will see his offspring and prolong his days, and the will of the Lord will prosper in his hands.

> **Questions**
>
> - Whose will was it for this to happen?
> - What was the life of Allah's Promised Servant made to be?
> - What happens to Allah's Promised Servant after his sacrificial death?
> - What does it mean that "the Lord makes his life an offering for sin"?

I discovered that Allah makes it clear within his complete revelation in the Holy Bible what all of this means. At this point when Allah revealed Isaiah chapter 53, the following points, however, were clear:

- In Allah's "will," the sufferings and death of Allah's Promised Servant were not failure but success.
- The "will" of Allah "will prosper in his hands." He will successfully accomplish Allah's will and plan.
- After the death of Allah's Promised Servant, Allah will "prolong his days."

Allah's Promised Savior

ISAIAH 53:11

"After he has suffered, he will see the light of life and be satisfied; by his knowledge my righteous servant will justify many, and he will bear their iniquities."

> **Questions**
>
> - What happens to Allah's Promised Servant in this verse?
> - How does all of this benefit humans?
> - How does Allah's Promised Servant and Savior accomplish that?

The end result of the sacrifice of Allah's Promised Servant is not defeat and death, but significant accomplishment as the Savior! Allah's "righteous servant will justify many."

Allah Honors the Servant and Savior

ISAIAH 53:12

Therefore I will give him a portion among the great, and he will divide the spoils with the strong, because he poured out his life unto death, and was numbered with the transgressors. For he bore the sin of many, and made intercession for the transgressors.

Please pause here and ponder what you've read.

- Explain the passages in your own words as if you were sharing it with someone else.
- Explain how the passages make you think or feel and why.
- What do the passages tell you about Allah?
- What do the passages tell you about you and your relationship with Allah?
- What action do you think Allah wants from you according to these passages?
- As a result, create an "I will . . ." statement to obey Allah according to these passages.

Allah Requires Substitutionary Sacrifice

Since humankind first sinned in Genesis 3 (which we discussed in chapter four of this book), Allah required a substitutionary blood sacrifice. Around 750 years prior to the revelations made in Isaiah 52–53, Allah revealed details of the required substitutionary animal sacrifice on The Day of Atonement in Leviticus 16 (which we reviewed in chapter seven of this book).

The sacrifice had to be a firstborn animal without defect, which atoned for the sins of the people. The substitutionary blood sacrifices symbolically and formally represented the forgiveness of the sins of the people of Allah. Only then could the people safely enter Allah's presence without dying.

Sacrifice of Allah's Servant

Then around 2,700 years ago, Allah revealed through the prophet Isaiah that there was to come a Servant and Savior who was without sin (like the firstborn animal without defect) to be the substitutionary blood sacrifice to carry the sins of the people. Allah's Servant and Savior was made an offering for sin.

In Isaiah, Allah reiterates this vital revelation fifteen times in just eight verses. In these words we see the substitutionary and voluntary nature of the sacrifice of his promised Servant and Savior:

ISAIAH 53:4

Surely he took up our pain ...

... and bore our suffering,"

ISAIAH 53:5

But he was pierced for our transgressions,

... he was crushed for our iniquities;

... the punishment that brought us peace was on him,

... and by his wounds we are healed.

ISAIAH 53:6

... and the Lord has laid on him the iniquity of us all.

ISAIAH 53:7

He was oppressed and afflicted, yet he did not open his mouth;

... he was led like a lamb to the slaughter, and as a sheep before its shearers is silent, so he did not open his mouth.

ISAIAH 53:8

... for the transgression of my people he was punished.

ISAIAH 53:10

... the Lord makes his life an offering for sin,

ISAIAH 53:11

... by his knowledge my righteous servant will justify many, and he will bear their iniquities.

ISAIAH 53:12

... he poured out his life unto death,

... For he bore the sin of many,

... and made intercession for the transgressors.

In the above verses, as well as the others we read in Isaiah chapter 52–53, Allah shares mysterious-sounding facts about His promised Servant and Savior. Although He has not yet explained the mystery, Allah will later on in the Holy Bible.

Chapter Conclusion

When I first read Isaiah chapters 52–53, it was difficult for me to grasp the full meaning. Also, I still had questions, like the following:

- Why can't Allah merely forgive humans to atone for their sins and restore them to Paradise?

- Why the need for a substitutionary blood sacrifice?
- Why the need for a Savior without sin?
- How can a Servant and Savior have victory not through personal, political, or military power, but through sacrifice?

Initially, these were all very strange, mysterious, and unclear concepts for me to consider. What was clear was that Allah required the blood of a substitutionary sacrifice that is without defect as atonement for sin. In these chapters in Isaiah, Allah promises a Servant Savior who will be the sacrifice—the atonement. But at first, I did not understand how that connected, if at all, to the blood sacrifice of a firstborn animal without defect.

As I continued in my journey through Allah's revelations in the Holy Bible, I discovered the connection that Allah makes clear. It is all part of Allah's loving, holy, righteous, complete, perfect, and most wonderful plan.

In the next chapter, we will study more of Allah's revelations about the Promised Servant and Savior. They are vital to leading you and me to the One and only Way that you and I can be restored to eternal Paradise with Allah. I am excited to continue this journey of discovery with you!

Will you pray that Allah will reveal the truth to you about His Word?

- What specific requests do you have for Allah now?
- If you have a Christian friend, then ask him or her to pray with you in the name of Jesus.
- If you do not know or have access to a Christian near you, then please contact us with your specific prayer request (pray@WordofAllah.org).

Be specific with any need or issue that Allah can do for you today, even if it is miraculous. It does not mean that Allah will perform a physical miracle for you. The greatest miracle Allah desires for you is eternal life in Paradise, and He has already accomplished that. In this book we study how you can have this greatest miracle from Allah. It is already yours if you choose it.

Jesus Heals Two Blind Men

MATTHEW 20:29-34

As Jesus and his disciples were leaving Jericho, a large crowd followed him. Two blind men were sitting by the roadside, and when they heard that Jesus was going by, they shouted, "Lord, Son of David, have mercy on us!"

The crowd rebuked them and told them to be quiet, but they shouted all the louder, "Lord, Son of David, have mercy on us!"

Jesus stopped and called them. "What do you want me to do for you?" he asked. "Lord," they answered, "we want our sight."

Jesus had compassion on them and touched their eyes. Immediately they received their sight and followed him.

Jesus Teaches about Judging Others

MATTHEW 7:1-5

"Do not judge, or you too will be judged. For in the same way you judge others, you will be judged, and with the measure you use, it will be measured to you.

"Why do you look at the speck of sawdust in your brother's eye and pay no attention to the plank in your own eye? How can you say to your brother, 'Let me take the speck out of your eye,'

when all the time there is a plank in your own eye? You hypocrite, first take the plank out of your own eye, and then you will see clearly to remove the speck from your brother's eye."

Jesus Teaches about False Prophets

MATTHEW 7:15-20

"Watch out for false prophets. They come to you in sheep's clothing, but inwardly they are ferocious wolves. By their fruit you will recognize them. Do people pick grapes from thorn bushes, or figs from thistles? Likewise, every good tree bears good fruit, but a bad tree bears bad fruit. A good tree cannot bear bad fruit, and a bad tree cannot bear good fruit. Every tree that does not bear good fruit is cut down and thrown into the fire. Thus, by their fruit you will recognize them."

The Greatest in Allah's Kingdom!

MATTHEW 18:1-5

At that time the disciples came to Jesus and asked, "Who, then, is the greatest in the kingdom of heaven?"

He called a little child to him, and placed the child among them. And he said: "Truly I tell you, unless you change and become like little children, you will never enter the kingdom of heaven. Therefore, whoever takes the lowly position of this child is the greatest in the kingdom of heaven. And whoever welcomes one such child in my name welcomes me."

Children and Jesus

MATTHEW 19:13-15

Then people brought little children to Jesus for him to place his hands on them and pray for them. But the disciples rebuked them.

Jesus said, "Let the little children come to me, and do not hinder them, for the kingdom of heaven belongs to such as these." When he had placed his hands on them, he went on from there.

The Self-Righteous Person and Allah's Kingdom

MATTHEW 19:16-30

Just then a man came up to Jesus and asked, "Teacher, what good thing must I do to get eternal life?"

"Why do you ask me about what is good?" Jesus replied. "There is only One who is good. If you want to enter life, keep the commandments."

"Which ones?" he inquired.

Jesus replied, "You shall not murder, you shall not commit adultery, you shall not steal, you shall not give false testimony, honor your father and mother, and love your neighbor as yourself."

"All these I have kept," the young man said. "What do I still lack?"

Jesus answered, "If you want to be perfect, go, sell your possessions and give to the poor, and you will have treasure in heaven. Then come, follow me." When the young man heard this, he went away sad, because he had great wealth.

Then Jesus said to his disciples, "Truly I tell you, it is hard for someone who is rich to enter the kingdom of heaven. Again I tell you, it is easier for a camel to go through the eye of a needle than for someone who is rich to enter the kingdom of God."

When the disciples heard this, they were greatly astonished and asked, "Who then can be saved?"

Jesus looked at them and said, "With man this is impossible, but with God (Allah) all things are possible."

Peter answered him, "We have left everything to follow you! What then will there be for us?"

Jesus said to them, "Truly I tell you, at the renewal of all things, when the Son of Man sits on his glorious throne, you who have followed me will also sit on twelve thrones, judging the twelve tribes of Israel. And everyone who has left houses or brothers or sisters or father or mother or wife or children or fields for my sake will receive a hundred times as much and will inherit eternal life. But many who are first will be last, and many who are last will be first."

Miracle for Muslim Boy

Years ago, my wife, Karen, and I went along with a small group of Christians to a part of a city where many Muslims live. We went there to share the love of Jesus with Muslims, and to pray for them in His name. As we were walking on the street, there was a young man pushing another in a wheelchair. We believed Allah wanted us to pray for the boy in the wheelchair. The teenager's name was "Ali," and his older brother was "Ahmad." Ali had not been able to walk since he was a child.

After getting to know them a little, we offered to pray for Ali in the name of Jesus. They accepted our offer. We, the small group of

Christians, wholeheartedly believed that Allah wanted to heal Ali. Each of us laid our hands on Ali and took turns praying in the name of Jesus for Allah to provide miraculous healing. But there was no miracle that day. We were all very disappointed. Ali and Ahmad accepted from us an audio Holy Bible to listen to Allah's Word.

A few years later, another small group of Christians went to that part of the city to share the love of Jesus with Muslims, and to pray for them in His name. The team saw Ahmad walking along, pushing Ali around in the wheelchair. They too offered to pray for Allah to miraculously heal Ali, in the name of Jesus. This time, Ali got up and walked! Ali, Ahmad, and the Christian team all praised Allah!

Ali and Ahmad now too know and believe in Allah's One and only Way to be saved.

Allah the Shepherd

PSALM 23

The Lord is my shepherd, I lack nothing.

He makes me lie down in green pastures, he leads me beside quiet waters, he refreshes my soul. He guides me along the right paths for his name's sake.

Even though I walk through the darkest valley, I will fear no evil, for you are with me; your rod and your staff, they comfort me.

You prepare a table before me in the presence of my enemies. You anoint my head with oil; my cup overflows. Surely your goodness and love will follow me all the days of my life, and I will dwell in the house of the Lord forever.

Chapter Eleven

Jesus

As always, let us begin with a prayer:

We pray that the Holy Spirit of Allah will fill us to reveal, guide, and teach us the truth as we discover Allah's Word and revelations in the Holy Bible. In Jesus's name, amen!

Up to this point in our study, we have been learning about some of Allah's progressive revelations about His One and only Way that you and I can be saved from hell and into eternal Paradise with Allah. As we continue on this exciting journey of discovering and understanding Allah's perfect plan, it is helpful to understand Allah's Word in the Holy Bible within a historical context.

In the previous chapter, we reviewed some of Allah's revelations about the Servant Savior that were delivered through the prophet Isaiah approximately 2,700 years ago. In the 250 years that followed, Allah delivered more revelations through 10[1] other prophets, and they are recorded in the Holy Bible. Then, for a period of about 460

---

[1] The 10 prophets after Isaiah were (all dates are approximate): Nahum, 660–630 B.C.; Zephaniah, 640–609 B.C.; Habakkuk, 640–609 B.C.; Daniel, 605–536 B.C.; Jeremiah, 600–550 B.C.; Ezekiel, 593–571 B.C.; Obadiah, 586–553 B.C.; Haggai, 520 B.C.; Zechariah, 520 B.C.; Malachi, 460 B.C.

years (between 2,460 to around 2,000 years ago), Allah chose not to reveal anything new through any prophet.

During the 460 years while Allah remained silent, the ancient nation of Israel was conquered repeatedly. For more than 1,000 years and through many of His prophets, Allah had predicted and warned the nation of Israel of the impending punishment for behaving like every other nation and straying from Him—the One and only Allah. Through these prophets Allah also had revealed around three hundred things about his promised Servant Savior through whom He would bring light and salvation to the world.

By around 2,000 years ago, religious people of the day understood from Allah's revelations that the promised Servant and Savior was due at any time. At that time, Allah's people of ancient Israel (Jews) were living under the rule and oppression of the Roman Empire. Aware that Allah's revelations promised a Savior to come as King, they anticipated a mighty warrior who would come and conquer their enemies and save them.

Then around 2,000 years ago, Allah spoke again. He revealed more Holy Scriptures until around 95 A.D. when the final revelations of His complete and perfect plan to save us were recorded. After we study some of these revelations in the next few chapters of this book, we will know and understand Allah's Way to restore us to Paradise.

In the next few pages, we will focus on some of Allah's revelations about Jesus. These revelations are essential to understanding Allah's One and only Way that you and I can be with Allah forever in Paradise. Together, we will look at the Holy Scriptures about Jesus's life and the predictions that were made about Him hundreds of years before he was born. As always, I encourage you to turn to and read the Holy Scriptures mentioned in our study.

Allah Sends Jibrail to Maryam and Foretells the Birth of Jesus

LUKE 1:26–33

In the sixth month of Elizabeth's pregnancy, God (Allah) sent the angel Gabriel (Jibrail in Arabic) to Nazareth, a town in Galilee, to a virgin pledged to be married to a man named Joseph (Yousef in Arabic), a descendant of David (Dawud in Arabic). The virgin's name was Mary (Maryam in Arabic). The angel went to her and said, "Greetings, you who are highly favored! The Lord is with you." Mary (Maryam) was greatly troubled at his words and wondered what kind of greeting this might be.

But the angel said to her, "Do not be afraid, Mary (Maryam); you have found favor with God (Allah). You will conceive and give birth to a son, and you are to call him Jesus. He will be great and will be called the Son of the Most High. The Lord God will give him the throne of his father David (Dawud), and he will reign over Jacob's (Yaqoub) descendants forever; his kingdom will never end."

The Virgin's Miraculous Conception

LUKE 1:34–38

"How will this be," Mary (Maryam) asked the angel, "since I am a virgin?"

The angel answered, "The Holy Spirit will come on you, and the power of the Most High will overshadow you. So the holy one to be born will be called the Son of God (Ibn Allah in Arabic). Even Elizabeth your relative is going to have a child in her old age, and she who was said to be unable to conceive is in her sixth month. For no word from God (Allah) will ever fail."

"I am the Lord's servant," Mary (Maryam) answered. *"May your word to me be fulfilled."*

Allah's Prediction—700 Years before the Virgin Birth of Jesus

ISAIAH 7:14

"Therefore the Lord himself will give you a sign: The virgin will conceive and give birth to a son, and will call him Immanuel."

Allah's Prediction Fulfilled

MATTHEW 1:18, 21–23

"This is how the birth of Jesus the Messiah (Al-Masih in Arabic) came about: His mother Mary (Maryam) was pledged to be married to Joseph (Yousef), but before they came together, she was found to be pregnant through the Holy Spirit . . . She will give birth to a son, and you are to give him the name Jesus, because he will save his people from their sins. All this took place to fulfill what the Lord had said through the prophet: 'The virgin will conceive and give birth to a son, and they will call him 'Immanuel' (which means "God (Allah) with us")."

Please pause here and ponder what you've read.

- Explain the passages in your own words as if you were sharing it with someone else.
- Explain how the passages make you think or feel and why.
- What do the passages tell you about Allah?

- What do the passages tell you about you and your relationship with Allah?
- What action do you think Allah wants from you according to these passages?
- As a result, create an "I will..." statement to obey Allah according to these passages.

The Birth of Jesus

LUKE 2:1-7

In those days Caesar Augustus issued a decree that a census should be taken of the entire Roman world. (This was the first census that took place while Quirinius was governor of Syria.) And everyone went to their own town to register.

So Joseph (Yousef) also went up from the town of Nazareth in Galilee to Judea, to Bethlehem the town of David (Dawud), because he belonged to the house and line of David (Dawud). He went there to register with Mary (Maryam), who was pledged to be married to him and was expecting a child. While they were there, the time came for the baby to be born, and she gave birth to her firstborn, a son. She wrapped him in cloths and placed him in a manger, because there was no guest room available for them.

Allah's Prediction—750 years before the Birth of Jesus

MICAH 5:2

"But you, Bethlehem Ephrathah, though you are small among the clans of Judah, out of you will come for me one who will be ruler over Israel, whose origins are from old, from ancient times."

Allah's Prediction Fulfilled

PLEASE TURN TO AND READ MATTHEW 2:4-6

When he had called together all the people's chief priests and teachers of the law, he asked them where the Messiah (Al-Masih) was to be born. "In Bethlehem in Judea," they replied, "for this is what the prophet has written: 'But you, Bethlehem, in the land of Judah, are by no means least among the rulers of Judah; for out of you will come a ruler who will shepherd my people Israel.'"

Good News!

LUKE 2:8-10

And there were shepherds living out in the fields nearby, keeping watch over their flocks at night. An angel of the Lord appeared to them, and the glory of the Lord shone around them, and they were terrified. But the angel said to them, "Do not be afraid. I bring you good news that will cause great joy for all the people."

Question

- Who was the good news for?

Al-Masih

LUKE 2:11-14:

"Today in the town of David (Dawud) a Savior has been born to you; he is the Messiah (Al-Masih), the Lord. This will be a sign to you: You will find a baby wrapped in cloths and lying in a manger." Suddenly a great company of the heavenly host appeared with the angel, praising God (Allah) and saying, "Glory to God (Allah) in the highest heaven, and on earth peace to those on whom his favor rests."

Question

- What is the good news?

Al-Masih, Allah's promised Savior, is the one to whom Allah has been pointing since humankind sinned. The One Allah had promised—through hundreds of predictions and revelations made for over a thousand years, through dozens of prophets—had finally arrived.

Sharing the Good News

LUKE 2:15–20

When the angels had left them and gone into heaven, the shepherds said to one another, "Let's go to Bethlehem and see this thing that has happened, which the Lord has told us about." So they hurried off and found Mary (Maryam) and Joseph (Yousef), and the baby, who was lying in the manger. When they had seen him, they spread the word concerning what had been told them about this child, and all who heard it were amazed at what the shepherds said to them.

But Mary (Maryam) treasured up all these things and pondered them in her heart. The shepherds returned, glorifying and praising God (Allah) for all the things they had heard and seen, which were just as they had been told.

Salvation and Light to the World

LUKE 2:25–32

Now there was a man in Jerusalem called Simeon, who was righteous and devout. He was waiting for the consolation of Israel, and the Holy Spirit was on him. It had been revealed to him by the Holy Spirit that he would not die before he had seen the Lord's Messiah (Al-Masih). Moved by the Spirit, he went into the temple courts. When the parents brought in the child Jesus to do for him what the custom of the Law required, Simeon took him in his arms and praised God (Allah), saying:

"Sovereign Lord, as you have promised, you may now dismiss your servant in peace. For my eyes have seen your salvation, which you have prepared in the sight of all nations: a light for revelation to the Gentiles, and the glory of your people Israel."

Allah's Revelations Fulfilled

Please read these two passages of Holy Scripture about Allah's revelations of his Promised Servant and Savior that Simeon was referring to from over 700 years before.

ISAIAH 49:6

"He says: 'It is too small a thing for you to be my servant to restore the tribes of Jacob and bring back those of Israel I have kept. I will also make you a light for the Gentiles, that my salvation may reach to the ends of the earth.'"

ISAIAH 52:10

The Lord will lay bare his holy arm in the sight of all the nations, and all the ends of the earth will see the salvation of our God (Allah).

Gentiles were any non-Israeli, non-Jewish people—in other words, the rest of the world. Allah's promised Servant and Savior was to bring "salvation" and "light" to the entire world, to "all the ends of the earth."

Foretold Opposition

LUKE 2:33-35

The child's father and mother marveled at what was said about him. Then Simeon blessed them and said to Mary (Maryam), his mother: "This child is destined to cause the falling and rising of many in Israel, and to be a sign that will be spoken against, so that the thoughts of many hearts will be revealed. And a sword will pierce your own soul too."

Questions

- Still under the influence of Allah's Holy Spirit, what predictions does Simeon share with the parents of Jesus?
- What do you think it means that Jesus will "be a sign that will be spoken against"?
- What do you think it means when Simeon says to the parents of Al-Masih that "a sword will pierce your own soul too"?
- What possible connections do you see in these Holy Scriptures to Allah's predictions about his suffering Servant/Savior from Isaiah chapters 52–53 that we reviewed in the previous chapter of this book?

A Prophetess Recognizes Jesus as Savior

LUKE 2:36–38

There was also a prophet, Anna, the daughter of Penuel, of the tribe of Asher. She was very old; she had lived with her husband seven years after her marriage, and then was a widow until she was eighty-four. She never left the temple but worshiped night and day, fasting and praying. Coming up to them at that very moment, she gave thanks to God (Allah) and spoke about the child to all who were looking forward to the redemption of Jerusalem.

Please pause here and ponder what you've read.

- Explain the passages in your own words as if you were sharing it with someone else.
- Explain how the passages make you think or feel and why.
- What do the passages tell you about Allah?
- What do the passages tell you about you and your relationship with Allah?
- What action do you think Allah wants from you according to these passages?
- As a result, create an "I will . . ." statement to obey Allah according to these passages.

Chapter Conclusion

When I arrived at these parts of my study of Allah's Word in the Holy Bible, it was clear that Allah was revealing that there is something uniquely special about Jesus. In summary of this chapter, Allah's revelations included:

- Jibril announcing the miraculous virgin conception of Jesus.

- Angels celebrating and praising Allah for Jesus.
- The fulfillment of the predictions about Jesus's birth that had been recorded in the Holy Scriptures in the preceding 1,500 years.
- Jesus is identified as the Servant Savior whom Allah predicted. He was the promised Messiah.
- The birth of Jesus was celebrated as Good News.
- Jesus was called the salvation and light of the world.

With all the above in mind, I realized that these are vital revelations from Allah. I also understood that my proper understanding and response to these Holy Scriptures would determine my eternal destination. So I continued the careful study of Allah's revelation.

In the next chapter of this book, we will study what Allah reveals about the last few years of the life of Jesus on earth. We will see that hundreds of predictions Allah made for nearly 1,500 years were fulfilled in and by Jesus. Additionally, we will see how these revelations fit into Allah's perfect plan to bring you and me back to eternal life in Paradise with Him. What we will read next concerns the most important event in history. It is an event upon which our eternity depends.

Will you pray that Allah will reveal the truth to you about His Word?

- What specific requests do you have for Allah now?
- If you have a Christian friend, then ask him or her to pray with you in the name of Jesus.
- If you do not know or have access to a Christian near you, then please contact us with your specific prayer request (pray@WordofAllah.org).

Be specific with any need or issue that Allah can do for you today, even if it is miraculous. It does not mean that Allah will perform a physical miracle for you. The greatest miracle Allah desires for you is eternal life in Paradise, and He has already accomplished that. In this book we study how you can have this greatest miracle from Allah. It is already yours if you choose it.

Miraculous Healing of Blind Man

MARK 8:22–26

They came to Bethsaida, and some people brought a blind man and begged Jesus to touch him. He took the blind man by the hand and led him outside the village. When he had spit on the man's eyes and put his hands on him, Jesus asked, "Do you see anything?"

He looked up and said, "I see people; they look like trees walking around."

Once more Jesus put his hands on the man's eyes. Then his eyes were opened, his sight was restored, and he saw everything clearly. Jesus sent him home, saying, "Don't even go into the village."

Al-Masih

MARK 8:27–30

Jesus and his disciples went on to the villages around Caesarea Philippi. On the way he asked them, "Who do people say I am?"

They replied, "Some say John the Baptist; others say Elijah; and still others, one of the prophets."

"But what about you?" he asked. "Who do you say I am?"

Peter answered, "You are the Messiah (Al-Masih)." Jesus warned them not to tell anyone about him.

Earthly Cost of Following Jesus

MARK 8:31-38

He then began to teach them that the Son of Man must suffer many things and be rejected by the elders, the chief priests and the teachers of the law, and that he must be killed and after three days rise again. He spoke plainly about this, and Peter took him aside and began to rebuke him.

But when Jesus turned and looked at his disciples, he rebuked Peter. "Get behind me, Satan!" he said. "You do not have in mind the concerns of God (Allah), but merely human concerns."

The he called the crowd to him along with his disciples and said:

"Whoever wants to be my disciple must deny themselves and take up their cross and follow me. For whoever wants to save their life will lose it, but whoever loses their life for me and for the gospel will save it. What good is it for someone to gain the whole world, yet forfeit their soul? Or what can anyone give in exchange for their soul? If anyone is ashamed of me and my words in this adulterous and sinful generation, the Son of Man will be ashamed of them when he comes in his Father's glory with the holy angels."

The Transfiguration

MARK 9:1-13

And he said to them, "Truly I tell you, some who are standing here will not taste death before they see that the kingdom of God (Allah) has come with power."

After six days Jesus took Peter, James and John with him and led them up a high mountain, where they were all alone. There he was transfigured before them. His clothes became dazzling white, whiter than anyone in the world could bleach them. And there appeared before them Elijah and Moses (Musa), who were talking with Jesus.

Peter said to Jesus, "Rabbi, it is good for us to be here. Let us put up three shelters—one for you, one for Moses (Musa) and one for Elijah." (He did not know what to say, they were so frightened.) Then a cloud appeared and covered them, and a voice came from the cloud: "This is my Son, whom I love. Listen to him!"

Suddenly, when they looked around, they no longer saw anyone with them except Jesus. As they were coming down the mountain, Jesus gave them orders not to tell anyone what they had seen until the Son of Man had risen from the dead. They kept the matter to themselves, discussing what "rising from the dead" meant. And they asked him, "Why do the teachers of the law say that Elijah must come first?"

Jesus replied, "To be sure, Elijah does come first, and restores all things. Why then is it written that the Son of Man must suffer much and be rejected? But I tell you, Elijah has come, and they have done to him everything they wished, just as it is written about him."

Boy Healed

MARK 9:14–29

When they came to the other disciples, they saw a large crowd around them and the teachers of the law arguing with them. As soon as all the people saw Jesus, they were overwhelmed with wonder and ran to greet him. "What are you arguing with them about?" he asked.

A man in the crowd answered, "Teacher, I brought you my son, who is possessed by a spirit that has robbed him of speech. Whenever it seizes him, it throws him to the ground. He foams at the mouth, gnashes his teeth and becomes rigid. I asked your disciples to drive out the spirit, but they could not."

"You unbelieving generation," Jesus replied, "how long shall I stay with you? How long shall I put up with you? Bring the boy to me."

So they brought him. When the spirit saw Jesus, it immediately threw the boy into a convulsion. He fell to the ground and rolled around, foaming at the mouth. Jesus asked the boy's father, "How long has he been like this?"

"From childhood," he answered. "It has often thrown him into fire or water to kill him. But if you can do anything, take pity on us and help us."

"'If you can'?" said Jesus. "Everything is possible for one who believes."

Immediately the boy's father exclaimed, "I do believe; help me overcome my unbelief!"

When Jesus saw that a crowd was running to the scene, he rebuked the impure spirit. "You deaf and mute spirit," he said, "I command you, come out of him and never enter him again."

The spirit shrieked, convulsed him violently and came out. The boy looked so much like a corpse that many said, "He's dead." But Jesus took him by the hand and lifted him to his feet, and he stood up. After Jesus had gone indoors, his disciples asked him privately, "Why couldn't we drive it out?"

He replied, "This kind can come out only by prayer."

Muslim Girl Has Miraculous Dream/Vision

A few years ago, my wife, Karen, and I went to an area where many Muslims live so we could share the love of Jesus with them and pray for them in His name. After a few hours, I felt very tired, so we decided it was time for us to leave. As we were walking, a teenage girl in a hijab ran toward Karen and me, calling out for us to wait.

I thought, *Lord, I feel too tired to talk with anyone else today. I just want to leave. What could the girl want?*

The girl said to me, with much enthusiasm, "My name is Khadijah, and I know you!"

I did not recognize her, so I said, "I'm so sorry, I don't remember ever meeting you before."

Khadijah replied, "We did not meet in person before, but you have been in my dreams for a long time."

When I asked her to explain what she meant, Khadijah told me she began having a recurring, vivid dream years ago. In the dream, Khadijah saw a being in the shape of a man dressed in dazzling white, whiter than anything she had ever seen. Around him shone the brightest light she had ever seen. Then a friendly-looking, smiling man appeared in the dream who would begin to tell her the identity of the being dressed in white, but she always woke up before the being's identity was revealed.

"You are that man in my dream who tells me who is glowing in white clothes!" Khadijah exclaimed.

Karen and I looked at each other and then at Khadijah in utter surprise. I silently looked at Khadijah while praying internally, *Lord, I've never had this happen to me before. I've heard about some Muslims having dreams and visions of you, but I have never explained the meaning to any of them before. Please guide me, Lord.*

"Jesus!" I heard in my head. "Jesus!"

In that moment, I thought of the Transfiguration passage we just read from Mark in the Holy Bible. So I told Khadijah that it was Jesus she was seeing in the dream. Khadijah went on to study much of Allah's revelations in the Holy Bible, as you and I are doing together. Eventually, Khadijah believed Allah's Word.

Insha'Allah, so will you.

O' Allah, Please Teach Me!

PSALM 25:1-12

In you, Lord my God, I put my trust.

I trust in you; do not let me be put to shame, nor let my enemies triumph over me.

No one who hopes in you will ever be put to shame, but shame will come to those who are treacherous without cause.

Show me your ways, Lord, teach me your paths.

Guide me in your truth and teach me, for you are God (Allah) my Savior, and my hope is in you all day long.

Remember, Lord, your great mercy and love, for they are from of old.

Do not remember the sins of my youth and my rebellious ways; according to your love remember me, for you, Lord, are good.

Good and upright is the Lord; therefore he instructs sinners in his ways.

He guides the humble in what is right and teaches them his way.

All the ways of the Lord are loving and faithful toward those who keep the demands of his covenant.

For the sake of your name, Lord, forgive my iniquity, though it is great.

Who, then, are those who fear the Lord? He will instruct them in the ways they should choose.

Chapter Twelve

Jesus
(Part Two)

As always, let us begin with a prayer:

We pray that the Holy Spirit of Allah will fill us to reveal, guide, and teach us the truth as we discover Allah's Word and revelations in the Holy Bible. In Jesus's name, amen!

Since humankind sinned and Allah removed us from Paradise, He has made hundreds of predictions in the Holy Bible designed to point us to His One and only Way back to Paradise. Jesus's birth alone fulfilled the many predictions Allah had made about the Servant Savior event in the nearly 1,500 preceding years. But the fulfillment of Allah's predictions didn't stop there! The revelations of the many miracles, stories, and teachings during the life of Jesus are found in these sections of the Holy Bible: Matthew, Mark, Luke, and John. In those passages of Scripture, we see how all of Allah's predictions about His Servant Savior were fulfilled in and by Jesus.

For our time together in this session, we will study Allah's revelations regarding the last events of the life of Jesus on earth. These remarkable events fulfill all of the predictions Allah made about this Savior from the very beginning of His revelations in the Holy Bible. These events are the most important parts of Allah's revelations about how you and I can be saved from hell and into eternal Paradise with Allah.

Again, this will require studying lots of Holy Scriptures. As always, it is worth it, since our understanding and response to these Scriptures will help determine our eternal destination.

Jesus Predicts His Death

MATTHEW 16:21–27

From that time on Jesus began to explain to his disciples that he must go to Jerusalem and suffer many things at the hands of the elders, the chief priests and the teachers of the law, and that he must be killed and on the third day be raised to life.

Peter took him aside and began to rebuke him. "Never, Lord!" he said. "This shall never happen to you!"

Jesus turned and said to Peter, "Get behind me, Satan! You are a stumbling block to me; you do not have in mind the concerns of God (Allah), but merely human concerns." Then Jesus said to his disciples, "Whoever wants to be my disciple must deny themselves and take up their cross and follow me. For whoever wants to save their life will lose it, but whoever loses their life for me will find it. What good will it be for someone to gain the whole world, yet forfeit their soul? Or what can anyone give in exchange for their soul? For the Son of Man is going to come in his Father's glory with his angels, and then he will reward each person according to what they have done."

Jesus (Part Two)

The death and resurrection of Jesus was so important that he tells his disciples about it again. When Jesus spoke these words, his followers didn't understand what He was talking about. Allah had a plan, and He revealed it again and again so that we, like Jesus's disciples, could eventually understand it.

> MATTHEW 17:22–23
>
> *When they came together in Galilee, he said to them, "The Son of Man is going to be delivered into the hands of men. They will kill him, and on the third day he will be raised to life." And the disciples were filled with grief.*

This event was so important that Allah revealed and had it recorded multiple times by different prophets.

> MATTHEW 20:17–19
>
> *Now Jesus was going up to Jerusalem. On the way, he took the Twelve aside and said to them, "We are going up to Jerusalem, and the Son of Man will be delivered over to the chief priests and the teachers of the law. They will condemn him to death and will hand him over to the Gentiles to be mocked and flogged and crucified. On the third day he will be raised to life!"*

Jesus comments on his death yet again, right before the event occurred.

> MATTHEW 26:1–5
>
> *When Jesus had finished saying all these things, he said to his disciples, "As you know, the Passover is two days away—and the Son of Man will be handed over to be crucified."*
>
> *Then the chief priests and the elders of the people assembled in the palace of the high priest, whose name was Caiaphas, and they schemed to arrest Jesus secretly and kill him. "But not*

during the festival," they said, "or there may be a riot among the people."

Now, let's read verses from Mark where Jesus predicts His death multiple times.

MARK 9:9–13:

As they were coming down the mountain, Jesus gave them orders not to tell anyone what they had seen until the Son of Man had risen from the dead. They kept the matter to themselves, discussing what "rising from the dead" meant. And they asked him, "Why do the teachers of the law say that Elijah must come first?"

Jesus replied, "To be sure, Elijah does come first, and restores all things. Why then is it written that the Son of Man must suffer much and be rejected? But I tell you, Elijah has come, and they have done to him everything they wished, just as it is written about him."

MARK 9:30–37

They left that place and passed through Galilee. Jesus did not want anyone to know where they were, because he was teaching his disciples. He said to them, "The Son of Man is going to be delivered into the hands of men. They will kill him, and after three days he will rise." But they did not understand what he meant and were afraid to ask him about it.

They came to Capernaum. When he was in the house, he asked them, "What were you arguing about on the road?" But they kept quiet because on the way they had argued about who was the greatest. Sitting down, Jesus called the Twelve and said, "Anyone who wants to be first must be the very last, and the servant of all." He took a little child whom he placed among them. Taking the child in his arms, he said to them, "Whoever welcomes one of these little children in my name welcomes me; and whoever welcomes me does not welcome me but the one who sent me."

Let's read Allah's revelations about Jesus's impending death as recorded in John.

JOHN 2:13–22

When it was almost time for the Jewish Passover, Jesus went up to Jerusalem. In the temple courts he found people selling cattle, sheep and doves, and others sitting at tables exchanging money. So he made a whip out of cords, and drove all from the temple courts, both sheep and cattle; he scattered the coins of the money changers and overturned their tables. To those who sold doves he said, "Get these out of here! Stop turning my Father's house into a market!"

His disciples remembered it is written: "Zeal for your house will consume me."

The Jews then responded to him, "What sign can you show us to prove your authority to do all this?"

Jesus answered them, "Destroy this temple, and I will raise it again in three days."

They replied, "It has taken forty-six years to build this temple, and you are going to raise it in three days?"

But the temple he had spoken of was his body. After he was raised from the dead, his disciples recalled what he had said. Then they believed the scripture and the words that Jesus had spoken.

JOHN 12:23-36

Jesus replied, "The hour has come for the Son of Man to be glorified. Very truly I tell you, unless a kernel of wheat falls to the ground and dies, it remains only a single seed. But if it dies, it produces many seeds. Anyone who loves their life will lose it, while anyone who hates their life in this world will keep it for eternal life. Whoever serves me must follow me; and where I am, my servant also will be. My Father will honor the one who serves me. Now my soul is troubled, and what shall I say? 'Father, save me from this hour'? No, it was for this very reason I came to this hour. Father, glorify your name!"

Then a voice came from heaven, "I have glorified it, and will glorify it again." The crowd that was there and heard it said it had thundered; others said an angel had spoken to him. Jesus said, "This voice was for your benefit, not mine. Now is the time for judgment on this world; now the prince of this world will be driven out. And I, when I am lifted up from the earth, will draw all people to myself."

He said this to show the kind of death he was going to die. The crowd spoke up, "We have heard from the Law that the Messiah (Al-Masih) will remain forever, so how can you say, 'The Son of Man must be lifted up'? Who is this 'Son of Man'?"

Then Jesus told them, "You are going to have the light just a little while longer. Walk while you have the light, before darkness overtakes you. Whoever walks in the dark does not know where they are going. Believe in the light while you have the light, so that you may become children of light." When he had finished speaking, Jesus left and hid himself from them.

Please pause here and ponder what you've read.

- Explain the passages in your own words as if you were sharing it with someone else.
- Explain how the passages make you think or feel and why.
- What do the passages tell you about Allah?
- What do the passages tell you about you and your relationship with Allah?
- What action do you think Allah wants from you according to these passages?
- As a result, create an "I will ..." statement to obey Allah according to these passages.

Jesus's Death

Now, let's read the account of the death of Jesus, as Allah reveals in Luke. For a couple of years leading up to this event, they had plotted and looked for opportunities to kill Jesus. Of course, as we've seen through His own predictions, Jesus already knew who was going to kill Him and when, so none of these events surprised Him. Then the right time came for Jesus to die, which was during the Passover.

The Plot to Kill Jesus

LUKE 22:1–6

Now the Festival of Unleavened Bread, called the Passover, was approaching, and the chief priests and the teachers of the law were looking for some way to get rid of Jesus, for they were afraid of the people. Then Satan entered Judas, called Iscariot, one of the Twelve. And Judas went to the chief priests and the officers of the temple guard and discussed with them how he might betray Jesus. They were delighted and agreed to give him money. He consented, and watched for an opportunity to hand Jesus over to them when no crowd was present.

The Last Supper

LUKE 22:14–37

When the hour came, Jesus and his apostles reclined at the table. And he said to them, "I have eagerly desired to eat this Passover with you before I suffer. For I tell you, I will not eat it again until it finds fulfillment in the kingdom of God (Allah)."

After taking the cup, he gave thanks and said, "Take this and divide it among you. For I tell you I will not drink again from the fruit of the vine until the kingdom of God (Allah) comes." And he took the bread, gave thanks and broke it, and gave it to them, saying, "This is my body given for you; do this in remembrance of me."

In the same way, after the supper he took the cup, saying, "This cup is the new covenant in my blood, which is poured out for you. But the hand of him who is going to betray me is with mine on the table. The Son of Man will go as it has been decreed. But woe to that man who betrays him!"

They began to question among themselves which of them it might be who would do this. A dispute also arose among them as to which of them was considered to be greatest. Jesus said to them, "The kings of the Gentiles lord it over them; and those who exercise authority over them call themselves Benefactors. But you are not to be like that. Instead, the greatest among you should be like the youngest, and the one who rules like the one who serves. For who is greater, the one who is at the table or the one who serves? Is it not the one who is at the table? But I am among you as one who serves. You are those who have stood by me in my trials. And I confer on you a kingdom, just as my Father conferred one on me, so that you may eat and drink at my table in my kingdom and sit on thrones, judging the twelve tribes of Israel. Simon, Simon, Satan has asked to sift all of you as wheat. But I have prayed for you, Simon, that your faith may not fail. And when you have turned back, strengthen your brothers."

But he replied, "Lord, I am ready to go with you to prison and to death."

Jesus answered, "I tell you, Peter, before the rooster crows today, you will deny three times that you know me." Then Jesus asked them, "When I sent you without purse, bag or sandals, did you lack anything?"

"Nothing," they answered.

He said to them, "But now if you have a purse, take it, and also a bag; and if you don't have a sword, sell your cloak and buy one. It is written: 'And he was numbered with the transgressors'; and I tell you that this must be fulfilled in me. Yes, what is written about me is reaching its fulfillment."

Jesus Prays

LUKE 22:39-46

Jesus went out as usual to the Mount of Olives, and his disciples followed him. On reaching the place, he said to them, "Pray that you will not fall into temptation." He withdrew about a stone's throw beyond them, knelt down and prayed, "Father, if you are willing, take this cup from me; yet not my will, but yours be done."

An angel from heaven appeared to him and strengthened him. And being in anguish, he prayed more earnestly, and his sweat was like drops of blood falling to the ground. When he rose from prayer and went back to the disciples, he found them asleep, exhausted from sorrow. "Why are you sleeping?" he asked them. "Get up and pray so that you will not fall into temptation."

Jesus Arrested

LUKE 22:47-53

While he was still speaking a crowd came up, and the man who was called Judas, one of the Twelve, was leading them. He approached Jesus to kiss him, but Jesus asked him, "Judas, are you betraying the Son of Man with a kiss?"

When Jesus' followers saw what was going to happen, they said, "Lord, should we strike with our swords?" And one of them struck the servant of the high priest, cutting off his right ear.

But Jesus answered, "No more of this!" And he touched the man's ear and healed him.

Then Jesus said to the chief priests, the officers of the temple guard, and the elders, who had come for him, "Am I leading a rebellion, that you have come with swords and clubs? Every day I was with you in the temple courts, and you did not lay a hand on me. But this is your hour—when darkness reigns."

Peter Disowns Jesus

LUKE 22:54-62

Then seizing him they led him away and took him into the house of the high priest. Peter followed at a distance. And when some there had kindled a fire in the middle of the courtyard and had sat down together, Peter sat down with them. A servant girl saw him seated there in the firelight. She looked closely at him and said, "This man was with him."

But he denied it. "Woman, I don't know him," he said.

A little later someone else saw him and said, "You also are one of them."

"Man, I am not!" Peter replied.

About an hour later another asserted, "Certainly this fellow was with him, for he is a Galilean."

Peter replied, "Man, I don't know what you're talking about!" Just as he was speaking, the rooster crowed. The Lord turned and looked straight at Peter. Then Peter remembered the word the Lord had spoken to him: "Before the rooster crows today, you will disown me three times." And he went outside and wept bitterly.

Please pause here and ponder what you've read.

- Explain the passages in your own words as if you were sharing it with someone else.
- Explain how the passages make you think or feel and why.
- What do the passages tell you about Allah?
- What do the passages tell you about you and your relationship with Allah?
- What action do you think Allah wants from you according to these passages?
- As a result, create an "I will . . ." statement to obey Allah according to these passages.

Soldiers Mock Jesus

LUKE 22:63-65

The men who were guarding Jesus began mocking and beating him. They blindfolded him and demanded, "Prophesy! Who hit you?" And they said many other insulting things to him.

The Question!

LUKE 22:66-70

At daybreak the council of the elders of the people, both the chief priests and the teachers of the law, met together, and Jesus was led before them. "If you are the Messiah (Al-Masih)," they said, "tell us."

Jesus answered, "If I tell you, you will not believe me, and if I asked you, you would not answer. But from now on, the Son of Man will be seated at the right hand of the mighty God (Allah)."

They all asked, "Are you then the Son of God (Allah)?"

He replied, "You say that I am."

Jesus Charged with Blasphemy

LUKE 22:71

Then they said, "Why do we need any more testimony? We have heard it from his own lips."

For additional important information about this exchange, let's review this story as Allah revealed it through Mark.

MARK 14:61-65

Again the high priest asked him, "Are you the Messiah (Al-Masih), the Son of the Blessed One?"

"I am," said Jesus. "And you will see the Son of Man sitting at the right hand of the Mighty One and coming on the clouds of heaven."

The high priest tore his clothes. "Why do we need any more witnesses?" he asked. "You have heard the blasphemy. What do you think?" They all condemned him as worthy of death. Then some began to spit at him; they blindfolded him, struck him with their fists, and said, "Prophesy!" And the guards took him and beat him.

Jesus was condemned for blasphemy. The religious leaders of His day had been wanting to kill Him for blasphemy for several years prior to that. For additional relevant information connected to these events, let's review Allah's revelation in John where Jesus was speaking in Jerusalem.

JOHN 10:22-39

Then came the Festival of Dedication at Jerusalem. It was winter, and Jesus was in the temple courts walking in Solomon's Colonnade. The Jews who were there gathered around him, saying, "How long will you keep us in suspense? If you are the Messiah (Al-Masih), tell us plainly."

Jesus answered, "I did tell you, but you do not believe. The works I do in my Father's name testify about me, but you do not believe because you are not my sheep. My sheep listen to my voice; I know them, and they follow me. I give them eternal life, and they shall never perish; no one will snatch them out of my hand. My Father, who has given them to me, is greater than all; no one can snatch them out of my Father's hand. I and the Father are one."

Again his Jewish opponents picked up stones to stone him, but Jesus said to them, "I have shown you many good works from the Father. For which of these do you stone me?"

"We are not stoning you for any good work," they replied, "but for blasphemy, because you, a mere man, claim to be God (Allah)."

Jesus answered them, "Is it not written in your Law, 'I have said you are "gods"'? If he called them 'gods,' to whom the word of God (Allah) came—and Scripture cannot be set aside—what about the one whom the Father set apart as his very own and sent into the world? Why then do you accuse me of blasphemy because I said, 'I am God's (Allah's) Son'? Do not believe me unless I do the works of my Father. But if I do them, even though you do not believe me, believe the works, that you may know and understand that the Father is in me, and I in the Father."

Again they tried to seize him, but he escaped their grasp.

Jesus with the Roman Ruler in Jerusalem

Let's resume Allah's revelation that we've been reading.

LUKE 23:1–7

Then the whole assembly rose and led him off to Pilate. And they began to accuse him, saying, "We have found this man subverting our nation. He opposes payment of taxes to Caesar and claims to be Messiah (Al-Masih), a king."

So Pilate asked Jesus, "Are you the king of the Jews?"

"You have said so," Jesus replied.

Then Pilate announced to the chief priests and the crowd, "I find no basis for a charge against this man."

But they insisted, "He stirs up the people all over Judea by his teaching. He started in Galilee and has come all the way here." On hearing this, Pilate asked if the man was a Galilean. When he learned that Jesus was under Herod's jurisdiction, he sent him to Herod, who was also in Jerusalem at that time.

Pilate, as a Roman ruler of the area, did not care about a religious blasphemy charge, nor did he believe in Allah. When Pilate failed to respond to their religious complaints, the Jewish leaders focused their attacks on things the Roman Empire would consider treason, which was punishable by death.

Jesus Ridiculed and Mocked

LUKE 23:8-12

When Herod saw Jesus, he was greatly pleased, because for a long time he had been wanting to see him. From what he had heard about him, he hoped to see him perform a sign of some sort. He plied him with many questions, but Jesus gave him no answer. The chief priests and the teachers of the law were standing there, vehemently accusing him.

Then Herod and his soldiers ridiculed and mocked him. Dressing him in an elegant robe, they sent him back to Pilate. That day Herod and Pilate became friends—before this they had been enemies.

In chapter ten of this book, we studied Allah's revelations about a promised Servant Savior in Isaiah 53. Allah's predictions are being fulfilled here. Jesus chooses to be silent, meek and humble, just as

Allah had revealed through Isaiah. The character of Jesus is completely different from what humans expected from a king. Just as He revealed in Isaiah, Allah was glorified through weakness.

Jesus Sentenced to Die

LUKE 23:13-25

Pilate called together the chief priests, the rulers and the people, and said to them, "You brought me this man as one who was inciting the people to rebellion. I have examined him in your presence and have found no basis for your charges against him. Neither has Herod, for he sent him back to us; as you can see, he has done nothing to deserve death. Therefore, I will punish him and then release him."

But the whole crowd shouted, "Away with this man! Release Barabbas to us!" (Barabbas had been thrown into prison for an insurrection in the city, and for murder.) Wanting to release Jesus, Pilate appealed to them again. But they kept shouting, "Crucify him! Crucify him!"

For the third time he spoke to them: "Why? What crime has this man committed? I have found in him no grounds for the death penalty. Therefore I will have him punished and then release him."

But with loud shouts they insistently demanded that he be crucified, and their shouts prevailed. So Pilate decided to grant their demand. He released the man who had been thrown into prison for insurrection and murder, the one they asked for, and surrendered Jesus to their will.

The Death Sentence Carried Out

LUKE 23:26-38

As the soldiers led him away, they seized Simon from Cyrene, who was on his way in from the country, and put the cross on him and made him carry it behind Jesus. A large number of people followed him, including women who mourned and wailed for him.

Jesus turned and said to them, "Daughters of Jerusalem, do not weep for me; weep for yourselves and for your children. For the time will come when you will say, 'Blessed are the childless women, the wombs that never bore and the breasts that never nursed!' Then they will say to the mountains, 'Fall on us!' and to the hills, 'Cover us!' For if people do these things when the tree is green, what will happen when it is dry?"

Two other men, both criminals, were also led out with him to be executed. When they came to the place called the Skull, they crucified him there, along with the criminals—one on his right, the other on his left. Jesus said, "Father, forgive them, for they do not know what they are doing."

And they divided up his clothes by casting lots. The people stood watching, and the rulers even sneered at him. They said, "He saved others; let him save himself if he is God's (Allah's) Messiah (Al-Masih), the Chosen One." The soldiers also came up and mocked him. They offered him wine vinegar and said, "If you are the king of the Jews, save yourself." There was a written notice above him, which read: This is the King of the Jews.

Jesus's Promise to a Criminal

LUKE 23:39-43

One of the criminals who hung there hurled insults at him: "Aren't you the Messiah (Al-Masih)? Save yourself and us!"

But the other criminal rebuked him. "Don't you fear God (Allah)," he said, "since you are under the same sentence? We are punished justly, for we are getting what our deeds deserve. But this man has done nothing wrong." Then he said, "Jesus, remember me when you come into your kingdom."

Jesus answered him, "Truly I tell you, today you will be with me in paradise."

Jesus Dies

LUKE 23:44-49

It was now about noon, and darkness came over the whole land until three in the afternoon, for the sun stopped shining. And the curtain of the temple was torn in two. Jesus called out with a loud voice, "Father, into your hands I commit my spirit." When he had said this, he breathed his last.

The centurion, seeing what had happened, praised God (Allah) and said, "Surely this was a righteous man." When all the people who had gathered to witness this sight saw what took place, they beat their breasts and went away. But all those who knew him, including the women who had followed him from Galilee, stood at a distance, watching these things.

Jesus Buried

LUKE 23:50–56

Now there was a man named Joseph, a member of the Council, a good and upright man, who had not consented to their decision and action. He came from the Judean town of Arimathea, and he himself was waiting for the kingdom of God (Allah). Going to Pilate, he asked for Jesus' body. Then he took it down, wrapped it in linen cloth and placed it in a tomb cut in the rock, one in which no one had yet been laid.

It was Preparation Day, and the Sabbath was about to begin. The women who had come with Jesus from Galilee followed Joseph and saw the tomb and how his body was laid in it. Then they went home and prepared spices and perfumes. But they rested on the Sabbath in obedience to the commandment.

The Resurrection of Jesus

LUKE 24:1–12

On the first day of the week, very early in the morning, the women took the spices they had prepared and went to the tomb. They found the stone rolled away from the tomb, but when they entered, they did not find the body of the Lord Jesus. While they were wondering about this, suddenly two men in clothes that gleamed like lightning stood beside them.

In their fright the women bowed down with their faces to the ground, but the men said to them, "Why do you look for the living among the dead? He is not here; he has risen! Remember how he told you, while he was still with you in Galilee: 'The Son of Man must be delivered over to the hands of sinners, be cru-

cified and on the third day be raised again.'" Then they remembered his words.

When they came back from the tomb, they told all these things to the Eleven and to all the others. It was Mary Magdalene, Joanna, Mary the mother of James, and the others with them who told this to the apostles. But they did not believe the women, because their words seemed to them like nonsense. Peter, however, got up and ran to the tomb. Bending over, he saw the strips of linen lying by themselves, and he went away, wondering to himself what had happened.

Please pause here and ponder what you've read.

- Explain the passages in your own words as if you were sharing it with someone else.
- Explain how the passages make you feel and why.
- What do the passages tell you about Allah?
- What do the passages tell you about you and your relationship with Allah?
- What action do you think Allah wants from you according to these passages?
- As a result, create an "I will..." statement to obey Allah according to these passages.

Allah's Scriptures Fulfilled!

LUKE 24:13–35

Now that same day two of them were going to a village called Emmaus, about seven miles from Jerusalem. They were talking with each other about everything that had happened. As they talked and discussed these things with each other, Jesus himself came up and walked along with them; but they were kept from recognizing him.

He asked them, "What are you discussing together as you walk along?"

They stood still, their faces downcast. One of them, named Cleopas, asked him, "Are you the only one visiting Jerusalem who does not know the things that have happened there in these days?"

"What things?" he asked.

"About Jesus of Nazareth," they replied. "He was a prophet, powerful in word and deed before God (Allah) and all the people. The chief priests and our rulers handed him over to be sentenced to death, and they crucified him; but we had hoped that he was the one who was going to redeem Israel. And what is more, it is the third day since all this took place. In addition, some of our women amazed us. They went to the tomb early this morning but didn't find his body. They came and told us that they had seen a vision of angels, who said he was alive. Then some of our companions went to the tomb and found it just as the women had said, but they did not see Jesus."

He said to them, "How foolish you are, and how slow to believe all that the prophets have spoken! Did not the Messiah (Al-Masih) have to suffer these things and then enter his glory?" And beginning with Moses (Musa) and all the Prophets, he explained to them what was said in all the Scriptures concerning himself.

As they approached the village to which they were going, Jesus continued on as if he were going farther. But they urged him strongly, "Stay with us, for it is nearly evening; the day is almost over." So he went in to stay with them.

When he was at the table with them, he took bread, gave thanks, broke it and began to give it to them. Then their eyes were opened and they recognized him, and he disappeared from their sight. They asked each other, "Were not our hearts burning within us while he talked with us on the road and opened the Scriptures to us?"

They got up and returned at once to Jerusalem. There they found the Eleven and those with them, assembled together and saying, "It is true! The Lord has risen and has appeared to Simon." Then the two told what had happened on the way, and how Jesus was recognized by them when he broke the bread.

Allah's Scriptures Must Be fulfilled!

LUKE 24:36-49

While they were still talking about this, Jesus himself stood among them and said to them, "Peace be with you."

They were startled and frightened, thinking they saw a ghost. He said to them, "Why are you troubled, and why do doubts rise in your minds? Look at my hands and my feet. It is I myself! Touch me and see; a ghost does not have flesh and bones, as you see I have."

When he had said this, he showed them his hands and feet. And while they still did not believe it because of joy and amazement, he asked them, "Do you have anything here to eat?" They gave him a piece of broiled fish, and he took it and ate it in their presence. He said to them, "This is what I told you while I was still with you: Everything must be fulfilled that is written about me in the Law of Moses (Musa), the Prophets and the Psalms."

Then he opened their minds so they could understand the Scriptures. He told them, "This is what is written: The Messiah (Al-Masih) will suffer and rise from the dead on the third day, and repentance for the forgiveness of sins will be preached in his name to all nations, beginning at Jerusalem. You are witnesses of these things. I am going to send you what my Father has promised; but stay in the city until you have been clothed with power from on high."

Jesus Ascends to Heaven

LUKE 24:50–53

When he had led them out to the vicinity of Bethany, he lifted up his hands and blessed them. While he was blessing them, he left them and was taken up into heaven. Then they worshiped him and returned to Jerusalem with great joy. And they stayed continually at the temple, praising God (Allah).

Please pause here and ponder what you've read.

- Explain the passages in your own words as if you were sharing it with someone else.
- Explain how the passages make you think or feel and why.
- What do the passages tell you about Allah?
- What do the passages tell you about you and your relationship with Allah?
- What action do you think Allah wants from you according to these passages?
- As a result, create an "I will . . ." statement to obey Allah according to these passages.

Chapter Conclusion

When I first read Allah's revelations about Jesus's death and his resurrection, I felt a complete sense of awe.

How are you feeling?

What are you thinking?

For me, it took time for the full weight of these revelations to sink in. It was a lot for me to process and comprehend. After all, through dozens of prophets for approximately 1,500 years, Allah had been pointing to Jesus, His death, and His resurrection. The events we just read about fulfilled the hundreds of predictions Allah had made regarding the Servant Savior—Jesus. The most important revelations of Allah's complete and perfect plan to save you and me from hell—and allow us eternal life in Paradise with Him—came to life in these Holy Scriptures.

Will you pray that Allah will reveal the truth to you about His Word?

- What specific requests do you have for Allah now?
- If you have a Christian friend, then ask him or her to pray with you in the name of Jesus.
- If you do not know or have access to a Christian near you, then please contact us with your specific prayer request (pray@WordofAllah.org).

Be specific with any need or issue that Allah can do for you today, even if it is miraculous. It does not mean that Allah will perform a physical miracle for you. The greatest miracle Allah desires for you is eternal life in Paradise, and He has already accomplished that. In this book we study how you can have this greatest miracle from Allah. It is already yours if you choose it.

Muslim Girl Prays for Miracle

"Murshida" had to flee her war-torn Islamic country with her teenage daughter, "Fatima." Murshida's husband, "Mustafa," remained behind to fight in the war. Fatima was born quadriplegic, paralyzed from the neck down. Murshida was Fatima's full-time caretaker and took her around in a wheelchair.

After fleeing their war-ravaged country, Murshida and Fatima lost all contact with Mustafa. The trauma of leaving their home and being separated from Mustafa was compounded by the fact that he provided the family's only source of income—and now they had lost that as well.

In a new country, living in very poor conditions, Murshida and Fatima heard about a place where Christians met to study the Holy Bible with Muslims and pray for them in the name of Jesus. They had heard reports of miraculous healings happening to Muslims there as a result of those prayers. Desperate for help and hope, Murshida took Fatima there to hear Allah's Word and to see if Allah would grant Fatima miraculous healing.

For weeks, Murshida took Fatima to meet with the Christians. They studied Allah's Word together, and the Christians prayed for healing for Fatima.

Karen and I met Murshida and Fatima at the meetings during one of my visits to the Middle East. They had been to the meetings a number of times, but Fatima had not been healed. The two women continued to come to study Allah's Word and ask for healing for Fatima. At every meeting they attended during the next few weeks, Karen and I, along with the other Christians there, prayed for Fatima in the name of Jesus.

But she was not healed.

One night, we studied the resurrection story, just as you read in this chapter. Afterward, as we always did following our studies, Karen and I asked who would like prayers in the name of Jesus. As usual, Murshida rushed Fatima to my wife and me for prayers. When we asked what, specifically, they wanted us to pray for, I expected to hear their usual response: healing for Fatima. This time, however, they surprised us.

Murshida and Fatima enthusiastically said, "We believe that Jesus is Lord and that Allah raised Him from the dead!"

They quoted from Romans 10:9: "If you declare with your mouth, 'Jesus is Lord,' and believe in your heart that God (Allah) raised him from the dead, you will be saved."

Karen and I celebrated with Murshida and Fatima, praising Allah that they had understood and believed His Word.

A few days later, Karen and I got shocking news: Fatima had become suddenly ill and died. We were filled with sorrow.

The next time I saw Murshida, she surprised us again when she said, "I am happy that Fatima believed in Jesus before she died. Because of that, she is now in Paradise with Allah, where there is no more suffering, pain, or sorrow. We all prayed for a physical miracle, which lasts only on earth. But Allah gave us an eternal spiritual miracle with Jesus."

Amen!

Chapter Thirteen

Allah

As always, let us begin with a prayer:
We pray that the Holy Spirit of Allah will fill us to reveal, guide, and teach us the truth as we discover Allah's Word and revelations in the Holy Bible. In Jesus's name, amen!

Up to this point in our study, we have read and learned about some of Allah's revelations. We have seen how His predictions that were delivered over a period of approximately 1,500 years through dozens of prophets were fulfilled by Jesus's birth, death, and resurrection as recorded in the Holy Scriptures.

Now we have arrived at that point in the Holy Bible where Allah reveals the One and only Way you and I can return to Paradise. Everything that is needed to accomplish Allah's perfect, complete, holy, righteous, and loving plan is finished, which means we can clearly understand what Allah requires. I am so excited that we have arrived at this moment in our study and cannot wait to share Allah's Word with you. Let's jump right in!

Allah's One and Only Way

We'll begin our study with Al-Masih (Jesus) revealing and explaining Allah's plan. Please turn to and read the following passages of the Holy Bible.

JOHN 3:12-18

"I have spoken to you of earthly things and you do not believe; how then will you believe if I speak of heavenly things? No one has ever gone into heaven except the one who came from heaven—the Son of Man. Just as Moses (Musa) lifted up the snake in the wilderness, so the Son of Man must be lifted up, that everyone who believes may have eternal life in him.

"For God (Allah) so loved the world that he gave his one and only Son, that whoever believes in him shall not perish but have eternal life. For God (Allah) did not send his Son (Al-Masih) into the world to condemn the world, but to save the world through him. Whoever believes in him (Jesus) is not condemned, but whoever does not believe stands condemned already because they have not believed in the name of God's (Allah's) one and only Son (Al-Masih)."

JOHN 3:31-36

"The one who comes from above is above all; the one who is from the earth belongs to the earth, and speaks as one from the earth. The one who comes from heaven is above all. He testifies to what he has seen and heard, but no one accepts his testimony. Whoever has accepted it has certified that God (Allah) is truthful. For the one whom God (Allah) has sent speaks the words of God (Allah), for God (Allah) gives the Spirit without limit."

"The Father loves the Son (Al-Masih) and has placed everything in his hands. Whoever believes in the Son (Al-Masih) has eternal life, but whoever rejects the Son (Al-Masih) will not see life, for God's (Allah's) wrath remains on them."

JOHN 14:6

Jesus answered, "I am the way and the truth and the life. No one comes to the Father except through me . . . "

Allah's Revelation Continues

ACTS 4:11–12

"Jesus is 'the stone you builders rejected, which has become the cornerstone.' Salvation is found in no one else, for there is no other name under heaven given to mankind by which we must be saved."

1 JOHN 5:10–12

Whoever believes in the Son (Ibn) of God (Allah) accepts this testimony. Whoever does not believe God (Allah) has made him out to be a liar, because they have not believed the testimony God (Allah) has given about his Son (Ibn). And this is the testimony: God (Allah) has given us eternal life, and this life is in his Son (Ibn). Whoever has the Son (Ibn) has life; whoever does not have the Son (Ibn) of God (Allah) does not have life.

Please pause here and ponder what you've read.

- Explain the passages in your own words as if you were sharing it with someone else.
- Explain how the passages make you think or feel and why.
- What do the passages tell you about Allah?

- What do the passages tell you about you and your relationship with Allah?
- What action do you think Allah wants from you according to these passages?
- As a result, create an "I will..." statement to obey Allah according to these passages.

Now, let's review more of Allah's revelations about His One and Only Way.

Who Jesus Is

The Bread of Life

JOHN 6:35, 40

Then Jesus declared, "I am the bread of life. Whoever comes to me will never go hungry, and whoever believes in me will never be thirsty.... For my Father's will is that everyone who looks to the Son (Ibn) and believes in him shall have eternal life, and I will raise them up at the last day."

JOHN 6:43–48

"Stop grumbling among yourselves," Jesus answered. "No one can come to me unless the Father who sent me draws them, and I will raise them up at the last day. It is written in the Prophets: 'They will all be taught by God (Allah).' Everyone who has heard the Father and learned from him comes to me. No one has seen the Father except the one who is from God (Allah); only he has seen the Father. Very truly I tell you, the one who believes has eternal life. I am the bread of life."

The Good Shepherd

JOHN 10:6-7

Jesus used this figure of speech, but the Pharisees did not understand what he was telling them. Therefore Jesus said again, "Very truly I tell you, I am the gate for the sheep."

JOHN 10:9

"I am the gate; whoever enters through me will be saved..."

JOHN 10:11

"I am the good shepherd. The good shepherd lays down his life for the sheep."

JOHN 10:14-18

"I am the good shepherd; I know my sheep and my sheep know me—just as the Father knows me and I know the Father—and I lay down my life for the sheep. I have other sheep that are not of this sheep pen. I must bring them also. They too will listen to my voice, and they shall be one flock and one shepherd.

"The reason my Father loves me is that I lay down my life—only to take it up again. No one takes it from me, but I lay it down of my own accord. I have authority to lay it down and authority to take it up again. This command I received from my Father."

The Messiah

JOHN 10:24-30

The Jews who were there gathered around him, saying, "How long will you keep us in suspense? If you are the Messiah (Al-Masih), tell us plainly."

Jesus answered, "I did tell you, but you do not believe. The works I do in my Father's name testify about me, but you do not believe because you are not my sheep. My sheep listen to my voice; I know them, and they follow me. I give them eternal life, and they shall never perish; no one will snatch them out of my hand. My Father, who has given them to me, is greater than all; no one can snatch them out of my Father's hand. I and the Father are one."

The Resurrection and Life

JOHN 11:17, 23–26

On his arrival, Jesus found that Lazarus had already been in the tomb for four days . . . Jesus said to her, "Your brother will rise again."

Martha answered, "I know he will rise again in the resurrection at the last day."

Jesus said to her, "I am the resurrection and the life. The one who believes in me will live, even though they die; and whoever lives by believing in me will never die. Do you believe this?"

JOHN 1:4

"In him was life, and that life was the light of all mankind."

Allah's Light

JOHN 1:4–9

In him was life, and that life was the light of all mankind. The light shines in the darkness, and the darkness has not overcome it. There was a man sent from God (Allah) whose name was John. He came as a witness to testify concerning that light, so that through him all might believe. He himself was not the light; he came only as a witness to the light. The true light that gives light to everyone was coming into the world.

JOHN 8:12

When Jesus spoke again to the people, he said, "I am the light of the world. Whoever follows me will never walk in darkness, but will have the light of life."

JOHN 12:44-46

Then Jesus cried out, "Whoever believes in me does not believe in me only, but in the one who sent me. The one who looks at me is seeing the one who sent me. I have come into the world as a light, so that no one who believes in me should stay in darkness."

The Lamb of Allah

JOHN 1:29

The next day John saw Jesus coming toward him and said, "Look, the Lamb of God (Allah), who takes away the sin of the world!"

1 PETER 1:18-19

For you know that it was not with perishable things such as silver or gold that you were redeemed from the empty way of life handed down to you from your ancestors, but with the precious blood of Christ (Al-Masih), a lamb without blemish or defect.

Allah's Word

JOHN 1:14A

The Word became flesh and made his dwelling among us.

REVELATION 19:13

He is dressed in a robe dipped in blood, and his name is the Word of God (Allah).

JOHN 1:14

The Word became flesh and made his dwelling among us. We have seen his glory, the glory of the one and only Son (Ibn), who came from the Father, full of grace and truth.

Allah Wants You to Believe in The Way

JOHN 6:28-29

Then they asked him, "What must we do to do the works God (Allah) requires?"

Jesus answered, "The work of God (Allah) is this: to believe in the one he has sent."

JOHN 20:30-31

Jesus performed many other signs in the presence of his disciples, which are not recorded in this book. But these are written that you may believe that Jesus is the Messiah (Al-Masih), the Son (Ibn) of God (Allah), and that by believing you may have life in his name.

ACTS 10:43

"All the prophets testify about him that everyone who believes in him receives forgiveness of sins through his name."

Please pause here and ponder what you've read.

- Explain the passages in your own words as if you were sharing it with someone else.
- Explain how the passages make you think or feel and why.
- What do the passages tell you about Allah?
- What do the passages tell you about you and your relationship with Allah?
- What action do you think Allah wants from you according to these passages?
- As a result, create an "I will . . ." statement to obey Allah according to these passages.

More Revelations to Consider about Jesus

Now, let's review a few more of Allah's revelations about His One and Only Way: Jesus Al-Masih.

Creator

JOHN 1:3

Through him all things were made; without him nothing was made that has been made.

Allah's revelation here is referring to Jesus Al-Masih.

Only One Judge and Savior!

ISAIAH 33:22

For the Lord is our judge, the Lord is our lawgiver, the Lord is our king; it is he who will save us.

JAMES 4:12A

There is only one Lawgiver and Judge, the one who is able to save and destroy...

Allah is the Judge, Lawgiver, King, and Savior. Also, Jesus Al-Masih says...

JOHN 5:19–21

Jesus gave them this answer: "Very truly I tell you, the Son (Al-Masih) can do nothing by himself; he can do only what he sees his Father doing, because whatever the Father does the Son (Ibn) also does. For the Father loves the Son (Ibn) and shows him all he does. Yes, and he will show him even greater works than these, so that you will be amazed. For just as the Father raises the dead and gives them life, even so the Son (Ibn) gives life to whom he is pleased to give it."

Allah revealed throughout the Holy Bible that there is only one Allah, one God, and it is He. We studied some of these verses in chapter three of this book. Allah also reveals in verses like the ones we just read in Isaiah and James that there is only one Savior, and it is the same Allah who is also the Judge. Al-Masih also states in the verses above that "the Son gives life to whom he is pleased to give it." And, as we studied in chapter ten of this book, Allah had foretold that He was sending a Savior.

JOHN 5:22–30, JESUS SAYS:

"Moreover, the Father judges no one, but has entrusted all judgment to the Son (Ibn), that all may honor the Son (Ibn) just as they honor the Father. Whoever does not honor the Son (Ibn) does not honor the Father, who sent him. Very truly I tell you, whoever hears my word and believes him who sent me has eternal life and will not be judged but has crossed over from death to life. Very truly I tell you, a time is coming and has now come when the dead will hear the voice of the Son (Ibn) of God (Allah) and those who hear will live.

"For as the Father has life in himself, so he has granted the Son also to have life in himself. And he has given him authority to judge because he is the Son of Man. Do not be amazed at this, for a time is coming when all who are in their graves will hear his voice and come out—those who have done what is good will rise to live, and those who have done what is evil will rise to be condemned. By myself I can do nothing; I judge only as I hear, and my judgment is just, for I seek not to please myself but him who sent me."

Allah revealed throughout the Holy Bible that there is only one Allah, one God, one Judge, one Savior, and it is He. When Al-Masih was on earth, He stated in the verses above that *"the Father judges no one, but has entrusted all judgment to the Son."*

MATTHEW 16:27, JESUS SAYS:

"For the Son of Man is going to come in his Father's glory with his angels, and then he will reward each person according to what they have done."

Moreover, Allah reveals this in 2 Corinthians 5:10:

"For we must all appear before the judgment seat of Christ (Al-Masih), so that each of us may receive what is due us for the things done while in the body, whether good or bad."

There is only One Allah, One God, One Judge, One Savior. Yet, Jesus Al-Masih is clearly these things as revealed by Allah. As I first read these things in the Holy Bible, I did not comprehend it fully. "How can all that be?" I asked Allah. So I prayed that Allah would help me understand. Then I continued to study Allah's revelations in the Holy Bible.

The One and Only I Am!

JOHN 8:57–59

"You are not yet fifty years old," they said to him, "and you have seen Abraham (Ibrahim)!"

"Very truly I tell you," Jesus answered, "before Abraham (Ibrahim) was born, I am!" At this, they picked up stones to stone him..."

The religious rulers of Al-Masih's time wanted to stone Him because He had just used the name Allah gave Himself, "I Am." Stoning was Allah's penalty for blasphemy. Adding to their anger and confusion, Al-Masih spoke those words while saying that He existed before Ibrahim was born—around 2,000 years prior to that time. That means Al-Masih was claiming to be eternal, something only Allah can be.

The following verses from Exodus, revealed by Allah around 3,500 years ago, give us the context of that statement of Al-Masih.

EXODUS 3:13-14

Moses (Musa) said to God (Allah), "Suppose I go to the Israelites and say to them, 'The God of your fathers has sent me to you,' and they ask me, 'What is his name?' Then what shall I tell them?"

God (Allah) said to Moses (Musa), "I AM WHO I AM. This is what you are to say to the Israelites: 'I AM has sent me to you.'"

When Al-Masih began His ministry on earth, He kept His true identity from most people, waiting until it was time for Him to die and then be resurrected to show Himself for who He was. As that time neared, Al-Masih began to confront His opponents and to increasingly reveal His true identity. The following Scriptures are an example:

JOHN 10:30-39

"I and the Father are one." Again, his Jewish opponents picked up stones to stone him, but Jesus said to them, "I have shown you many good works from the Father. For which of these do you stone me?"

"We are not stoning you for any good work," they replied, "but for blasphemy, because you, a mere man, claim to be God (Allah)."

Jesus answered them, "Is it not written in your Law, 'I have said you are "gods"'? If he called them 'gods,' to whom the word of God (Allah) came—and Scripture cannot be set aside—what about the one whom the Father set apart as his very own and sent into the world? Why then do you accuse me of blasphemy because I said, 'I am God's (Allah's) Son (Ibn)'? Do not believe me unless I do the works of my Father. But if I do them, even though you do not believe me, believe the works, that you may know and understand that the Father is in me, and I in the Father."

Again they tried to seize him, but he escaped their grasp.

They wanted to kill Al-Masih because what He said is the equivalent of Him stating that he is Allah. Al-Masih referred to Allah as Father and as Son. Al-Masih also referred to Himself as Son of Man (title for Allah), and also as Son of Allah. All these references to Himself as Allah were confusing to everyone—Al-Masih's disciples/followers and His opponents. It was a very difficult concept for them to comprehend, just as it was for me when I first began to read and study the Holy Scriptures. But as I studied more of Allah's revelations, and prayed to have His Spirit guide me, things became clearer.

Allah—the First and the Last!

Around 750 years prior to the birth of Al-Masih, Allah revealed the following in Isaiah.

ISAIAH 41:4

"Who has done this and carried it through, calling forth the generations from the beginning? I, the Lord—with the first of them and with the last—I am he."

ISAIAH 44:6

"This is what the Lord says—Israel's King and Redeemer, the Lord Almighty: I am the first and I am the last; apart from me there is no God."

ISAIAH 48:12

"Listen to me, Jacob, Israel, whom I have called: I am he; I am the first and I am the last."

Around sixty years after Al-Masih had returned to heaven, Allah reveals the following as part of His last set of revelations to end the Holy Bible.

REVELATION 1:8, AL-MASIH SAYS:

"I am the Alpha and the Omega," says the Lord God, "who is, and who was, and who is to come, the Almighty."

REVELATION 1:17–18, THE PROPHET QUOTES AL-MASIH:

When I saw him, I fell at his feet as though dead. Then he placed his right hand on me and said: "Do not be afraid. I am the First and the Last. I am the Living One; I was dead, and now look, I am alive for ever and ever! And I hold the keys of death and Hades."

REVELATION 2:8, AL-MASIH SAYS:

"To the angel of the church in Smyrna write: These are the words of him who is the First and the Last, who died and came to life again."

Revelation 22, the last chapter of Allah's Holy Scriptures, in verses 12–16, Al-Masih says:

"Look, I am coming soon! My reward is with me, and I will give to each person according to what they have done. I am the Alpha and the Omega, the First and the Last, the Beginning and the End.

Blessed are those who wash their robes, that they may have the right to the tree of life and may go through the gates into the city. Outside are the dogs, those who practice magic arts, the sexually immoral, the murderers, the idolaters and everyone who loves and practices falsehood.

I, Jesus, have sent my angel to give you this testimony for the churches. I am the Root and the Offspring of David, and the bright Morning Star."

Allah Is . . .

JOHN 1:1–2

In the beginning was the Word, and the Word was with God (Allah), and the Word was God (Allah). He was with God (Allah) in the beginning.

JOHN 1:14

The Word became flesh and made his dwelling among us. We have seen his glory, the glory of the one and only Son (Ibn), who came from the Father, full of grace and truth.

JOHN 1:18

No one has ever seen God (Allah), but the one and only Son (Ibn), who is himself God (Allah) and is in closest relationship with the Father, has made him known.

Please pause here and ponder what you've read.

- Explain the passages in your own words as if you were sharing it with someone else.
- Explain how the passages make you think or feel and why.
- What do the passages tell you about Allah?
- What do the passages tell you about you and your relationship with Allah?
- What action do you think Allah wants from you according to these passages?

- As a result, create an "I will . . ." statement to obey Allah according to these passages.

Chapter Conclusion

I had many questions when I first read and studied the Holy Scriptures that I shared with you in this chapter of the book. I wondered . . .

- How can Allah be only One, yet be revealed to us as Father and Son?
- How can Christians believe in a Triune Allah, or a Trinity, which is Father, Son, and the Holy Spirit, yet only One Allah?
- How can a tiny, finite human like me comprehend Allah, who is eternal and infinite?

The concept of Allah and Al-Masih being One was a very difficult concept for me to grasp or understand. I prayed and fasted. I wholeheartedly sought answers to understand who Allah is and what these Holy Scriptures revealed. Eventually, I concluded that it is not possible for a human to fully understand. Faith is required. In the end, without full comprehension, I, like all humans must at some point in their lives, had to decide what to believe. Even the right knowledge about Allah, along with logic and reasoning, is not adequate. Belief requires faith.

As I concluded that I could never fully understand the greatness and complexity of Allah, He comforted me with promises from the Holy Scriptures:

DEUTERONOMY 4:29

" . . . seek the Lord your God, you will find him if you seek him with all your heart and with all your soul."

JEREMIAH 29:13

"You will seek me and find me when you seek me with all your heart."

MATTHEW 7:7–8

". . . seek and you will find; knock and the door will be opened to you. For everyone who asks receives; the one who seeks finds; and to the one who knocks, the door will be opened."

So one day as I sat to pray, seeking to know Allah better, I looked up at the skies above me. I began thinking deeply about Allah's creation, the universe. I sensed Allah telling me how much evidence He has given us about triune (meaning three in one) things. After all, the universe is triune—space, time, and matter. Three things, one universe.

Space is triune: height, width, and depth. If you are spending this time with me by reading a printed book, everything in the book has height, width, and depth.

Solid, liquid, and gas are three physical states of matter.

Past, present, and future—all three are time. While you read this sentence, you experienced all three.

Space, matter, and time = universe. 1 x 1 x 1 = 1.

Father, Son, Holy Spirit = One Allah.

As I contemplated such things, I sensed Allah telling me that there are no created things that can adequately describe the Infinite Creator. But there are many things in Allah's vast creation, like the universe itself, that give us evidence of a Triune Allah. In that moment I began to try to contemplate Allah even deeper. Allah always was, always is, and always will be, without beginning or end.

I felt as if my head were going to explode. I felt like a tiny ant trying to absorb the mysteries of the universe with my tiny brain. I humbly acknowledged that I cannot possibly understand fully. But

I felt comfort that Allah provided many things in His creation that point us to the Creator, the Triune Allah.

Then Allah reminded me that He also provided all the necessary information we need in the Holy Bible in remarkable ways. After all, as a just Allah, He inspired the entire Holy Bible through forty prophets and messengers (most of whom never met or knew each other) on three continents over a period of approximately 1,575 years. Yet the entire Holy Bible forms a complete revelation that fits together perfectly, revealing the One and only Way for our salvation.

I found comfort in the ample evidence, whether in creation, or in the Holy Bible, or the peaceful assurance the Holy Spirit gave me in my heart, to reasonably believe in the Triune, One Allah. It had become clear that the one and only work that matters whether on Judgment Day one enters heaven or hell is if a person believes in Jesus Al-Masih, as is revealed in John 6:28–29:

> *"Then they asked him, 'What must we do to do the works (plural) God (Allah) requires?' Jesus answered, 'The work (singular) of God (Allah) is this: to believe in the one he has sent.'"*

With plenty of evidence, and a little bit of faith, I believed! I still had questions for Allah:

- Why did Allah have to come to earth as a human being known as Jesus Al-Masih, the Son of Allah, to live a sinless life, die on the Cross, and be resurrected, in order for humankind to be redeemed?
- Why did it have to be that way as the One and only Way?
- Why couldn't Allah just say we're forgiven?

In the next chapter we are ready to study the part of Allah's revelation in the Holy Bible that helps us comprehend His complete, perfect, just, holy, and loving plan to save you and me.

Let us close this session with special prayers, a little different than how we closed other sessions.

- Will you pray that the Holy Spirit of Allah reveal the truth to you about His Word?
- Will you pray that He helps you accept the truth?
- After all, the Holy Spirit of Allah revealing the truth to you and preparing your heart to accept it is the most important miracle, because it will determine your eternal destination.
- If you have a Christian friend, then ask him or her to pray with you in the name of Jesus Al-Masih.
- If you do not know or have access to a Christian near you, then please contact us with your specific prayer request (pray@WordofAllah.org).

Chapter Fourteen

The Why

As always, let us begin with a prayer:

We pray that the Holy Spirit of Allah will fill us to reveal, guide, and teach us the truth as we discover Allah's Word and revelations in the Holy Bible. In Jesus's name, amen!

I pray Allah's One and only Way by which you and I can be redeemed has become clearer as we have studied Allah's revelations in the Holy Bible together. What we learned in the previous chapter is of the utmost importance; in fact, the one and only work that matters on Judgment Day—the one thing that determines whether one enters Paradise or hell—is whether one believes in Jesus Al-Masih as Savior.

As Allah reveals in John 6:28–29, heartfelt belief is what He wants from each of us, *"Then they asked him, 'What must we do to do the works (plural) God (Allah) requires?' Jesus answered, 'The work (singular) of God (Allah) is this: to believe in the one he has sent.'"*

In this chapter, we will study Allah's revelation in the Holy Bible regarding the following questions:

- Why did Allah have to come to earth as a human being known as Jesus Al-Masih, the Son of Allah, to live a sinless life,

die on the cross, and be resurrected, in order for humankind to be redeemed?
- Why did it have to be that way as the One and only Way?
- Why couldn't Allah just say we are forgiven and allow everyone entry into Paradise?

I pray that our study will help you, as it did me, comprehend Allah's complete, perfect, just, holy, righteous, merciful, and loving plan to redeem you and me into eternal Paradise with Him.

Allah's Way Before the Resurrection of Al-Masih

As we studied together earlier in this book, Allah began implementing His salvation plan for you and me as soon as Adam and Hawa sinned in Genesis 3. We saw that He immediately revealed His plan and Way for salvation, which included sacrifice. We also studied passages from Exodus where Allah saved the people of ancient Israel from the death penalty of His righteous judgment with the blood sacrifice of the Passover lamb.

In chapter eight of this book, we learned that Allah commanded the people He had just redeemed from slavery to offer ongoing blood sacrifices of firstborn male animals without defect (Exodus 13). Later, in Leviticus, Allah reveals that forgiveness of sin and human atonement with Allah required ongoing blood sacrifices, and that without those sacrifices, humans could not survive the presence of the most holy Allah.

Neither could just anyone enter Allah's presence. Notice Allah's special instructions in Numbers 18:7 to Harun, whom Allah called as ancient Israel's first high priest: *"But only you and your sons may serve as priests in connection with everything at the altar and inside the curtain. I am giving you the service of the priesthood as a gift. Anyone else who comes near the sanctuary is to be put to death."* But even the high priest, the chosen mediator between Allah and His people, had to be cleansed by a blood sacrifice in order to survive the Presence of Allah in the Most Holy Place and offer atoning sacrifices on behalf of the people.

Allah's Way after Resurrection of Al-Masih

In chapters ten through twelve of this book we studied Allah's revelations in the Holy Bible that tied together the 1,500 years' worth of Holy Scripture and showed us that they all pointed to Al-Masih. Jesus Al-Masih is the Promised Servant Savior, the Lamb of Allah "who takes away the sin of the world" (John 1:29).

The Eternal High Priest

Let us now review a little more of Allah's revelations about His Way after the Sacrifice and Resurrection of Jesus Al-Masih. Please turn to and read the following verses:

HEBREWS 7:23–28

Now there have been many of those priests, since death prevented them from continuing in office; but because Jesus lives forever, he has a permanent priesthood. Therefore he is able to save completely those who come to God (Allah) through him, because he always lives to intercede for them.

Such a high priest truly meets our need—one who is holy, blameless, pure, set apart from sinners, exalted above the heavens. Unlike the other high priests, he does not need to offer sacrifices day after day, first for his own sins, and then for the sins of the people. He sacrificed for their sins once for all when he offered himself. For the law appoints as high priests men in all their weakness; but the oath, which came after the law, ap-

pointed the Son (Jesus Al-Masih), who has been made perfect forever.

Jesus Al-Masih is the supreme and eternal High Priest, the supreme and eternal Sacrifice because He is Allah. He came into the created physical world as a man, the Son of Allah, in order to do what only Allah could do. That's why Jesus Al-Masih is Allah's One and only Way to be saved.

Temporary Way before Al-Masih

HEBREWS 9:1

Now the first covenant had regulations for worship and also an earthly sanctuary.

HEBREWS 9:6–10

When everything had been arranged like this, the priests entered regularly into the outer room to carry on their ministry. But only the high priest entered the inner room, and that only once a year, and never without blood, which he offered for himself and for the sins the people had committed in ignorance.

The Holy Spirit was showing by this that the way into the Most Holy Place had not yet been disclosed as long as the first tabernacle was still functioning. This is an illustration for the present time, indicating that the gifts and sacrifices being offered were not able to clear the conscience of the worshiper. They are only a matter of food and drink and various ceremonial washings—external regulations applying until the time of the new order.

As Allah revealed in sections of the Holy Bible like Leviticus, the "tabernacle" was the earthly place of worship that also symbolized Allah's special presence with the people. Allah instructed that the high priest first had to sacrifice the blood sin offering outside the tabernacle. After the blood sacrifices, then throughout the year any of the priests could enter "regularly into the outer room."

Once a year, the high priest alone was allowed to enter the inner room (also known as the Most Holy Place), which was separated by a curtain (also referred to as the veil) from the rest of the tabernacle. The high priest could never enter this holy place without the blood of the sin offering. This sacrificial blood enabled him to safely pass through, enter, and survive the presence of Allah in the Most Holy Place.

After Jesus Al-Masih accomplished the work of the Savior required by Allah's perfect, holy, and righteous Law, Allah revealed the One and only Way back to Paradise into His holy presence.

Eternal Way through Jesus Al-Masih—The Only Perfect Tabernacle

HEBREWS 9:11-12

But when Christ (Al-Masih) came as high priest of the good things that are now already here, he went through the greater and more perfect tabernacle that is not made with human hands, that is to say, is not a part of this creation. He did not enter by means of the blood of goats and calves; but he entered the Most Holy Place once for all by his own blood, thus obtaining eternal redemption.

Question
- What does the "more perfect tabernacle" mean?

Let us review a couple of Holy Scriptures for the answer:

JOHN 2:18–21

The Jews then responded to him, "What sign can you show us to prove your authority to do all this?"

Jesus answered them, "Destroy this temple, and I will raise it again in three days."

They replied, "It has taken forty-six years to build this temple, and you are going to raise it in three days?" But the temple he had spoken of was his body.

Within this context, read the following in Colossians 2:9–10: "For in Christ (Al-Masih) all the fullness of the Deity lives in bodily form, and in Christ (Al-Masih) you have been brought to fullness. He is the head over every power and authority."

Since Jesus Al-Masih is Allah, He is the One and only Way that can satisfy all of Allah's loving, perfect, complete, holy, lawful, righteous, and just requirements. The previous earthly temples symbolically represented Allah's presence with the people. And the people could only live through that after they completed the temporary, imperfect, symbolic ceremonial requirements. All these religious rituals symbolically pointed humankind to the One and only perfect and eternal temple, which is Jesus Al-Masih.

Also, please remember that only the high priest could enter the Most Holy Place, and only after making the blood sacrifices exactly as commanded by Allah. Otherwise, he would die. After Jesus Al-Masih sacrificed His own blood on the cross, He entered the Most Holy Place (representing Allah's heavenly dwelling) for eternity.

Question

- What does the verse Hebrews 9:12 mean when it says, "obtaining eternal redemption"?

In the English dictionary, *forgive* means "to cancel a debt." That is different than *redemption*, which means "the action of regaining or gaining possession of something in exchange for payment, or clearing a debt."

Now let us gain a fuller understanding of atonement. To *atone* means "to make reparation." *Atonement* means "reparation for a wrong or injury." *Reparation* means "the making of amends for a wrong one has done, by paying money to or otherwise helping those who have been wronged"; it also means "the compensation for damage caused by the individual that caused it."

So from Allah's revelations in the Holy Bible, for atonement to happen, there has to be forgiveness plus redemption. In Hebrews 9:12, we see that Jesus Al-Masih is the One and only Way for complete and "eternal redemption." The blood of Al-Masih is the One and only Way of "obtaining" complete and eternal atonement between Allah and humankind.

Eternal Provision through Jesus Al-Masih

HEBREWS 9:13–22

The blood of goats and bulls and the ashes of a heifer sprinkled on those who are ceremonially unclean sanctify them so that they are outwardly clean. How much more, then, will the blood of Christ (Al-Masih), who through the eternal Spirit offered himself unblemished to God (Allah), cleanse our consciences from acts that lead to death, so that we may serve the living God (Allah)!

For this reason Christ (Al-Masih) is the mediator of a new covenant, that those who are called may receive the promised eternal inheritance—now that he has died as a ransom to set them free from the sins committed under the first covenant. In the case of a will, it is necessary to prove the death of the one who made it, because a will is in force only when somebody has died; it never takes effect while the one who made it is living.

This is why even the first covenant was not put into effect without blood. When Moses (Musa) had proclaimed every command of the law to all the people, he took the blood of calves, together with water, scarlet wool and branches of hyssop, and sprinkled the scroll and all the people. He said, "This is the blood of the covenant, which God (Allah) has commanded you to keep."

In the same way, he sprinkled with the blood the tabernacle and everything used in its ceremonies. In fact, the law requires that nearly everything be cleansed with blood, and without the shedding of blood there is no forgiveness.

Allah is the One and only Lawgiver, as He revealed in the Holy Bible. In Allah's perfect, complete, righteous, and just Law, the punishment for sin is death. That is because what is imperfect and unholy cannot coexist with what is perfect and holy. Allah is the One and only Judge. He determines our eternal destination, whether heaven or hell. Humankind sinned, therefore Allah within His Law had to sentence us to death and cast us out of Paradise.

But Allah loves you, me, and indeed, all of humankind. Because of His love, Allah had a perfect, complete, righteous, just, and loving way within his Law to pay for the sin debt and make redemption, thus making atonement for us. Allah accomplished all that within his Law by entering humankind as a human, the Son of Allah, Jesus

Al-Masih. Then He "died as a ransom" for us. As a result, the legal and valid requirements of Allah's Law were met.

Before Jesus Al-Masih accomplished this redemption permanently, Allah allowed the required penalty for sin to be delayed under temporary provisions. These tactics (the sacrifice of animals) were only found acceptable by Allah if the people followed every instruction Allah commanded. But with Al-Masih, Allah provided the One and only eternal provision that met all of the legal and valid requirements of Allah's Law.

The One and Only True and Eternal Way

HEBREWS 9:23–28

It was necessary, then, for the copies of the heavenly things to be purified with these sacrifices, but the heavenly things themselves with better sacrifices than these. For Christ (Al-Masih) did not enter a sanctuary made with human hands that was only a copy of the true one; he entered heaven itself, now to appear for us in God's (Allah's) presence.

Nor did he enter heaven to offer himself again and again, the way the high priest enters the Most Holy Place every year with blood that is not his own. Otherwise Christ (Al-Masih) would have had to suffer many times since the creation of the world. But he has appeared once for all at the culmination of the ages to do away with sin by the sacrifice of himself.

Just as people are destined to die once, and after that to face judgment, so Christ (Al-Masih) was sacrificed once to take away the sins of many; and he will appear a second time, not to bear sin, but to bring salvation to those who are waiting for him.

It was necessary for Al-Masih to sacrifice Himself, since He is Allah, as the One and only all-sufficient eternal sacrifice. Jesus Al-Masih is the One and only atoning sacrifice that can save/redeem a person from eternal punishment on Judgment Day. Throughout the book of Hebrews in the Holy Bible, Allah reveals a contrast between Jesus Al-Masih and every other way that people tried to gain access to Him. Nothing compares to His Eternal Way, which is why our eternal destination is determined by one simple thing: belief about and faith in Jesus Al-Masih as Savior.

Since you and I are finite, created beings, it is not possible for us to fully dive into all the dimensions or fully comprehend all this. We cannot grasp the greatness of it, or the wisdom, the love, the grace that is in it all. But what we can see clearly in Allah's Holy Word is that the One Way to restore us to Paradise is Jesus Al-Masih because Allah is the greatest and only eternal One.

In the end, each of us must have a measure of faith to believe and accept the Truth.

Please pause here and ponder what you've read.

- Explain the passages in your own words as if you were sharing it with someone else.
- Explain how the passages make you feel and why.
- What do the passages tell you about Allah?
- What do the passages tell you about you and your relationship with Allah?
- What action do you think Allah wants from you according to these passages?
- As a result, create an "I will . . ." statement to obey Allah according to these passages.

Allah's Unchanging Nature

Allah is sovereign, meaning when we as humans do not understand Allah's ways or actions, we typically understand that as Allah doing His will as he pleases. But there are things Allah cannot do, as per His own revelations. Let us review some of the ones relevant to answering the above questions of this chapter of the book.

Allah Cannot Do the Following

HEBREWS 6:18

... it is impossible for God (Allah) to lie...

NUMBERS 23:19

"God (Allah) is not human, that he should lie, nor a human being, that he should change his mind. Does he speak and then not act? Does he promise and not fulfill?"

DEUTERONOMY 32:4

"He is the Rock, his works are perfect, and all his ways are just. A faithful God who does no wrong, upright and just is he."

PSALM 89:34

"I will not violate my covenant or alter what my lips have uttered."

JOB 8:3

"Does God (Allah) pervert justice? Does the Almighty pervert what is right?"

DEUTERONOMY 1:17A

"Do not show partiality in judging; hear both small and great alike. Do not be afraid of anyone, for judgment belong to God."

ROMANS 2:11

For God (Allah) does not show favoritism.

JAMES 2:1, 9–10

My brothers and sisters, believers in our glorious Lord Jesus Christ (Al-Masih) must not show favoritism ... But if you show favoritism, you sin and are convicted by the law as lawbreakers. For whoever keeps the whole law and yet stumbles at just one point is guilty of breaking all of it.

Allah Is and Does...

PSALM 7:11A

God (Allah) is a righteous Judge...

PSALM 50:6

And the heavens proclaim his righteousness, for He is a God (Allah) of justice.

1 PETER 1:15–16

But just as He who called you is holy, so be holy in all you do; for it is written: "Be holy, because I am holy."

PSALM 18:30

As for God (Allah), his way is perfect: The Lord's word is flawless; he shields all who take refuge in him.

The Picture Is Bigger Than What We See

Allah is Creator of everything and everyone, including unseen things and beings. Allah is also a righteous Judge over *all*, which means there are more perspectives to consider than our human reality. This truth means that everything He does, including how He responds to sin and ungodliness, reflects who He is—not only to humankind but also to all of creation, including the invisible realms.

Let us peek a little into what Allah reveals into the invisible realms.

Allah's Invisible Realms

COLOSSIAN 1:16A

For in him all things were created: things in heaven and on earth, visible and invisible, whether thrones or powers or rulers or authorities ...

1 Kings 22:19b, where Allah gave a glimpse into the heavenly throne:

"... I saw the Lord sitting on his throne with all the multitudes of heaven standing around him on his right and on his left."

Isaiah 6:1–3, where Allah gave a glimpse into the heavenly throne:

... I saw the Lord, high and exalted, seated on a throne; and the train of his robe filled the temple. Above him were seraphim, each with six wings: With two wings they covered their faces, with two they covered their feet, and with two they were flying. And they were calling to one another: "Holy, holy, holy is the Lord Almighty; the whole earth is full of his glory."

In Revelation chapter 4 Allah gave the prophet a glimpse into heaven:

After this I looked, and there before me was a door standing open in heaven ... At once I was in the Spirit, and there before me was a throne in heaven with someone sitting on it ...

Surrounding the throne were twenty-four other thrones, and seated on them were twenty-four elders ... In the center, around the throne, were four living creatures ... Day and night they never stop saying: "Holy, holy, holy is the Lord God Almighty, who was, and is, and is to come."

Whenever the living creatures give glory, honor and thanks to him who sits on the throne and who lives for ever and ever, the twenty-four elders fall down before him who sits on the throne and worship him who lives for ever and ever. They lay their crowns before the throne and say: "You are worthy, our Lord and God, to receive glory and honor and power, for you created all things, and by your will they were created and have their being."

REVELATION 7:11-1

All the angels were standing around the throne and around the elders and the four living creatures. They fell down on their faces before the throne and worshiped God, saying: "Amen! Praise and glory and wisdom and thanks and honor and power and strength be to our God for ever and ever. Amen!"

Allah does not reveal to us how many types or numbers of created beings there are in the invisible/spiritual realm. But, through very short references in the Holy Bible, there appear to be many, even countless, beings that we cannot see with our mortal eyes.

Satan and Evil Spirits

EPHESIAN 6:12

For our struggle is not against flesh and blood, but against the rulers, against the authorities, against the powers of this dark world and against the spiritual forces of evil in the heavenly realms.

Revelation 12:7–9, where Allah gave the prophet a glimpse into a spiritual world:

Then war broke out in heaven. Michael and his angels fought against the dragon, and the dragon and his angels fought back. But he was not strong enough, and they lost their place in heaven. The great dragon was hurled down—that ancient serpent called the devil, or Satan, who leads the whole world astray. He was hurled to the earth, and his angels with him.

Allah gives us tiny glimpses throughout the Holy Bible on Satan and his sin against Allah. Sin entered creation through Satan. Allah also gives us tiny glimpses into Satan's angels, referred to as evil spirits and demons. Through a symbolic verse, Christian theologians believe one third of the original angels followed Satan and sinned against Allah.

Allah judged Satan and all the angels that sinned. Allah implemented the temporary penalty of kicking Satan and his followers out of heaven to the earth, and He will carry out the everlasting penalty on Judgment Day. Meanwhile, here is a glimpse of what they are allowed to do until then:

JOB 1:6

One day the angels came to present themselves before the Lord, and Satan also came with them.

Jesus Al-Masih tells his disciples:

LUKE 22:31

"Simon, Simon, Satan has asked to sift all of you as wheat."

ZECHARIAH 3:1

Then he showed me Joshua the high priest standing before the angel of the Lord, and Satan standing at his right side to accuse him.

REVELATION 12 (PARTS OF VERSES 9–10):

The great dragon was hurled down—that ancient serpent called the devil, or Satan, who leads the whole world astray. He was hurled to the earth, and his angels with him … For the accuser of our brothers and sisters, who accuses them before our God day and night, has been hurled down.

1 PETER 5:8

Be alert and of sober mind. Your enemy the devil prowls around like a roaring lion looking for someone to devour.

Here is a glimpse into what Allah will do with Satan, his demons, and all evil spirits on Judgment Day.

MATTHEW 25:41

"Then he will say to those on his left, 'Depart from me, you who are cursed, into the eternal fire prepared for the devil and his angels.'"

REVELATION 20:10

And the devil, who deceived them, was thrown into the lake of burning sulfur, where the beast and the false prophet had been thrown. They will be tormented day and night for ever and ever.

2 PETER 2:4

For if God (Allah) did not spare angels when they sinned, but sent them to hell, putting them in chains of darkness to be held for judgment…

Sin and Death Enter the World

ROMANS 5:12B

... sin entered the world through one man, and death through sin, and in this way death came to all people, because all sinned.

Since sin and shame entered the world through Adam, billions of created beings have suffered and died. That will include all who will be sentenced to hell on Judgment Day. Countless numbers of created beings will be judged on Judgment Day. The type of Judge Allah is will be on full display with all of them, including the accuser, Satan.

Please pause here and ponder what you've read.

- Explain the passages in your own words as if you were sharing it with someone else.
- Explain how the passages make you think or feel and why.
- What do the passages tell you about Allah?
- What do the passages tell you about you and your relationship with Allah?
- What action do you think Allah wants from you according to these passages?
- As a result, create an "I will . . ." statement to obey Allah according to these passages.

The Just and the Unjust Judge

Years ago I read a report about a high ranking, influential, and powerful judge in an Islamic country. The law in that country stated that if a person owed money, they must pay it back. If a person could not pay it back, they were to be imprisoned until they or someone on their behalf made full restitution by paying the money back.

The judge's son, "Kasab," used the power and credibility of his father's name to extort millions of dollars from many people. Kasab hid the money in financial accounts in foreign countries and bought properties there.

Many people from whom Kasab coerced money were left destitute. When Kasab's evil practices were brought to light, the law required him to offer financial restitution to his victims; but Kasab simply fled the country, never to return.

Kasab's father, the judge, eventually used his power and influence to have his son "forgiven." None of the people Kasab extorted money from ever received restitution for the what they had lost.

> **Questions**
> - How would you describe Kasab's father, the judge?
> - Did he show mercy? Forgiveness? Love?
> - Was he a righteous, just, or trustworthy judge?
> - What could he have done to be a righteous, just, and trustworthy judge?

This judge showed favoritism to his son. To be a righteous, just, and trustworthy judge who also showed true love, mercy, and forgiveness, the judge also needed to make atonement and restitution to restore everything back to the victims.

Unfortunately, we all know of other corrupt judges, politicians, and other people in influential and powerful positions.

But Allah is Creator of everything and everyone, including unseen things and beings. Allah is also the One and only Lawgiver. His Law is perfect, complete, righteous, just, and holy. Within Allah's Law, the penalty for sin is separation from Him. That is because what is imperfect and unholy cannot coexist with what is perfect and holy.

On Judgment Day, Allah's perfect, righteous, holy, yet merciful, graceful, forgiving, and loving character will be on full display with all created beings, seemingly countless in number. The temporary provisions for created beings will end, and each created being will be judged and sent to their eternal destination, whether heaven or hell, as required by the legal and valid requirements of Allah's Law.

Questions

- How does Allah reveal He will make atonement and restitution and redeem and transform you and me so that we can enter eternal Paradise with Him?

How will Allah accomplish all that while being a perfect, complete, holy, just, righteous, merciful, forgiving, gracious, and loving Judge to countless created beings and humankind?

In addition to what we have already covered in this chapter, let us review another one of Allah's revelations to help answer these questions.

ROMANS 3:21–26

But now apart from the law the righteousness of God (Allah) has been made known, to which the Law and the Prophets testify. This righteousness is given through faith in Jesus Christ (Al-Masih) to all who believe. There is no difference between Jew and Gentile, for all have sinned and fall short of the glory of God (Allah), and all are justified freely by his grace through the redemption that came by Christ Jesus.

God (Allah) presented Christ (Al-Masih) as a sacrifice of atonement, through the shedding of his blood—to be received by faith. He did this to demonstrate his righteousness, because in his forbearance he had left the sins committed beforehand unpunished—he did it to demonstrate his righteousness at the present time, so as to be just and the one who justifies those who have faith in Jesus.

When I originally read this passage, it was difficult for me to grasp its depth. With that in mind ...

Please pause here and ponder what you've read.

- Explain the passages in your own words as if you were sharing it with someone else.
- Explain how the passages make you think or feel and why.
- What do the passages tell you about Allah?
- What do the passages tell you about you and your relationship with Allah?
- What action do you think Allah wants from you according to these passages?
- As a result, create an "I will . . ." statement to obey Allah according to these passages.

Questions on Allah's revelation in Romans 3:21–26:

- How many times does Allah point to His righteousness?
- How did Allah make His "righteousness ... known"?
- How is "this righteousness ... given"?
- How are all, you and me, "justified" and redeemed?
- How do all, you and me, receive Allah's justification and "redemption"?
- Why did Allah present "Christ (Al-Masih) as a sacrifice of atonement"?

Allah reveals throughout the Holy Scriptures that all human beings, you and me, need righteousness, justification, grace, and redemption from Allah. No human being, neither you nor me, can attain any of that on our own. In Romans 3:21–26, we read that Allah freely gives all that through His One and only Way, Jesus Al-Masih. Every human being, you and me, "who believe" in Jesus Al-Masih, can receive Allah's gift.

After Allah entered His physical creation as the Son of Allah, He made it clear that all His revelations through all prophets and all Holy Scriptures pointed to Jesus Al-Masih. Before Al-Masih, it was impossible for humans to meet the righteous and perfect standard required by a holy Allah. "But now" that Al-Masih met the conditions of Allah's righteousness, "all are justified freely by his grace through the redemption that came by Christ Jesus."

Jesus Al-Masih is the righteousness of Allah, the promised Savior, eternal High Priest, and One and only Way provided by Allah, to freely give you and me His righteousness for justification. You and I can receive it only "through faith in Jesus Christ (Al-Masih)." It was the all-sufficient blood sacrifice of Jesus Al-Masih as the One and only perfect Lamb of Allah, and His resurrection, that made our redemption to Paradise possible.

An Unrighteous Judge

Kasab's father was an unrighteous judge. He abused his power and authority to protect his son. There was no justice, atonement, or restitution with the victims who lost much. Let us contrast that with Allah as Judge.

A Righteous Judge

Sin entered creation when Satan sinned. Then sin entered the physical world when Adam sinned. As a result, countless sinful unholy beings were kicked out of heaven. Also, human beings were removed from Paradise, and billions so far throughout history have suffered and died on earth. That will continue to happen until Judgment Day. Then countless unholy beings and humans will be punished in hell, eternally separated from a holy Allah. I cannot fathom the magnitude of shame and suffering that began with one sin. Can you?

How can anything, even a righteous Judge, make atonement, restitution, transformation, and redemption for all that?

In contrast to Kasab's father, the unrighteous judge, who protected his son at the expense of others, read what Jesus says in John 3:16 about Allah the Righteous Judge:

> "For God (Allah) so loved the world that he gave his one and only Son, that whoever believes in him shall not perish but have eternal life."

Allah demonstrated his love by allowing the Son to do what only He could have done and accomplished with His perfect, voluntary sacrifice.

Allah did not need to enter humanity as the Son, suffer, then die as a criminal on the Cross. When Jesus Al-Masih was being shamed, humiliated, and beaten, He could have just merely thought of killing the people doing that to Him and they would have been dead. Instead, Jesus Al-Masih endured the torture, the pain, and the humiliation.

Why would Allah endure all that? Why would He allow humans to treat Him that way?

Because Allah is love (1 John 4:16), and He loves you and me that much.

Can you fathom that type of love?

No human story or illustration can adequately demonstrate or communicate the magnitude of what infinite Allah did to save finite humankind, you and me. But we can look at our own human relationships to get a glimpse of the love Allah feels for us—His creation. With that in mind, here's a story to illustrate a human need, and how my loving human father met my need.

When I was a teenager, I committed a criminal offense and was put in jail. In order to get out of jail, I had to pay a monetary penalty. But I did not have money. There was nothing I could do to earn enough money to pay the penalty and get out of jail. I was stuck in prison. Someone else had to pay the penalty if I was going to get out of jail. I needed someone to save me.

My parents did not have enough money to pay my penalty either. They could have left me in jail to suffer the consequences. Instead, my parents gathered all the money they had, then sold assets they had until there was enough money to pay the penalty.

After the full payment was confirmed to the judge, he instructed me on a list of parole conditions to which I had to agree. Otherwise, he would not release me from jail. The conditions included counseling, with the goal of growing my character so I could learn to make wiser choices and mature into a better young man. After I accepted the conditions and agreed to obey the instructions, I was released from jail.

My parents did not have to sacrifice their finances to pay my penalty. But they did because they loved me. They believed that as I accepted and obeyed the parole conditions and instructions, I would grow and mature to have a better future. My parents helped make my freedom possible and created the conditions to make a better future for me possible.

In order to get out of jail, hope to change, and have a better future, I had to accept the financial sacrifice from my parents, and the judge's conditions of the parole.

Allah does that for you and me.

The situation and legal penalty I had as a teenager was nothing in comparison to the spiritual one you and I have with Allah. As per Allah's revelations in the Holy Bible, the sin of humankind has caused unfathomable shame, suffering, and death. The just penalty for that is hell. Humankind and all created beings can never adequately pay the infinite penalty, make atonement, restitution, and redeem our way out of hell and into Paradise with Allah.

Only Allah, who is One, and who created and sustains everything, could have paid the countless blood debt and satisfied the immeasurable legal requirement for eternity.

What Jesus Al-Masih did with His sacrifice on the cross was perfect and complete. Everything intersected in the one event. Allah's perfect, complete, just, righteous, holy, fair, and legal requirements of the Law were met. That intersected with Allah's perfect, complete, trustworthy, merciful, forgiving, gracious, fair, and infinitely loving character.

Allow me to paraphrase Romans 3:21–26: Allah "demonstrated his righteousness" by presenting "Christ (Al-Masih) as a sacrifice of atonement, through the shedding of his blood." Allah, who is infinite and loving, paid the legal and just penalty that human beings, you and I, can never have enough to pay. Allah paid the price so you and I can be legally and justly released from shame, death, and hell on Judgment Day.

As a result of the work of Allah in Jesus Al-Masih, Allah's "righteousness is given through faith in Jesus Christ (Al-Masih) to all who believe." Now, everyone, you and me, can be "justified freely by his grace through the redemption that came by Christ Jesus."

Allah did all that "to demonstrate his righteousness at the present time, so as to be just and the one who justifies those who have faith in Jesus."

Allah's own infinitely perfect and holy character could do no less.

Islam and Christianity Opposites in This

When I first studied Allah's revelations in the Holy Bible, before I accepted and put my "faith in Jesus," I realized that regarding the way to heaven, Islam and Christianity are exactly the opposite. I mentioned this early on in our studies together, but I would like to once again compare these differences.

The prophet Muhammad said he received a revelation from archangel Jibril over a period of twenty-three years while he was alone. Regarding Jesus Al-Masih, Islam denies that He is Allah, which is exactly the opposite of the revelations of the Holy Bible.

The Holy Bible is Allah-breathed through forty different prophets and messengers, most of whom did not personally know each other, over a period of nearly 1,575 years, on three different continents. Even through this span of time and breadth of messengers, the Holy Bible forms a complete story that fits together perfectly. In the Holy Bible, Allah repeatedly declares through these hundreds of years through various prophets as witnesses that His Word is perfect, flawless, endures forever, and will never pass away.

Also, Allah's Word in the Holy Bible reveals that Jesus Al-Masih is Allah; that Allah came as a human, Immanuel (meaning Allah with us), also called the Son of Man, the Son of Allah, the Word, the Savior; that Jesus Al-Masih is the One and only Way that meets all of Allah's requirements for forgiveness, atonement, restitution, and redemption. Believing (trusting) in Jesus Al-Masih is the One and only Way you and I can be justified back into Paradise.

I prayed wholeheartedly to Allah to guide me, and for Allah's Holy Spirit to reveal the truth about Jesus Al-Masih. Islam and the Holy Bible are exactly the opposite about this crucial belief that carries eternal implications. It was clear that my eternal destination depended on that decision.

I made the choice to believe Allah's Word, the Holy Bible. I accepted Allah's gift of eternal salvation available only in and through Jesus Al-Masih.

What will you choose to believe?

Will you pray that the Holy Spirit of Allah reveal the truth to you about Jesus Al-Masih?

- Will you pray that the Holy Spirit of Allah helps you accept the truth about Jesus Al-Masih?
- After all, your belief and response to this truth, the One and only Truth that matters, determines your eternal destination.
- If you have a Christian friend, then ask him or her to pray with you in the name of Jesus Al-Masih.
- If you do not know or have access to a Christian near you, then please contact us with your specific prayer request (pray@WordofAllah.org).

Are you willing to accept Allah's revelation that you "are justified freely by his grace through the redemption that came by Christ Jesus"?

Are you ready to receive Jesus Al-Masih as your salvation gift from Allah?

If so, then take the next step and do what Allah commands in Romans 10:9:

> .. declare with your mouth, "Jesus is Lord."
>
> Believe in your heart that God (Allah) raised him from the dead.

If you just did that, then Allah promises in Romans 10:9b–11:

> ... you will be saved. For it is with your heart that you believe and are justified, and it is with your mouth that you profess your faith and are saved. As Scripture says, "Anyone who believes in him will never be put to shame."

If you have chosen to believe and confess that Jesus Al-Masih is Lord and your salvation gift from Allah, I encourage you to repeat this prayer and meditate on what Allah has done for you.

Lord Jesus, I confess to you that I am a sinner who needs your forgiveness. I believe that you died for my sins, and now I want to turn away (repent) from (of) them. I ask you to enter my heart and my life. I put my trust and faith in you as my Savior. I promise to follow you as Lord of all my life. Thank you, Lord, because you saved me. Allah, I pray this in Jesus's name. Amen.

Chapter Fifteen

The End Times

As always, let us begin with a prayer:
We pray that the Holy Spirit of Allah will fill us to reveal, guide, and teach us the truth as we discover Allah's Word and revelations in the Holy Bible. In Jesus's name, amen!

*I*n this final chapter of this book, we will study a few of Allah's revelations about what He expects once a person believes in Jesus Al-Masih as Lord and Savior.

Let us begin, however, by reviewing some of Allah's revelations about the end times, Judgment Day, and the return to eternal Paradise with Allah.

Jesus Al-Masih Coming Again

ACTS 1:7–11

He (Jesus) said to them: "It is not for you to know the times or dates the Father has set by his own authority. But you will receive power when the Holy Spirit comes on you; and you will be *my witnesses in Jerusalem, and in all Judea and Samaria, and to the ends of the earth."*

After he said this, he was taken up before their very eyes, and a cloud hid him from their sight. They were looking intently up into the sky as he was going, when suddenly two men dressed in white stood beside them. "Men of Galilee," they said, "why do you stand here looking into the sky? This same Jesus, who has been taken from you into heaven, will come back in the same way you have seen him go into heaven."

HEBREWS 9:27-28

Just as people are destined to die once, and after that to face judgment, so Christ (Al-Masih) was sacrificed once to take away the sins of many; and he will appear a second time, not to bear sin, but to bring salvation to those who are waiting for him.

The Dead in Al-Masih

1 THESSALONIANS 4:13-18

Brothers and sisters, we do not want you to be uninformed about those who sleep in death, so that you do not grieve like the rest of mankind, who have no hope. For we believe that Jesus died and rose again, and so we believe that God (Allah) will bring with Jesus those who have fallen asleep in him. According to the Lord's word, we tell you that we who are still alive, who are left until the coming of the Lord, will certainly not precede those who have fallen asleep.

For the Lord himself will come down from heaven, with a loud command, with the voice of the archangel and with the trumpet call of God (Allah), and the dead in Christ (Al-Masih) will rise first. After that, we who are still alive and are left will be caught up together with them in the clouds to meet the Lord in the air. And so we will be with the Lord forever. Therefore encourage one another with these words.

1 CORINTHIANS 15:20-26

But Christ (Al-Masih) has indeed been raised from the dead, the firstfruits of those who have fallen asleep. For since death came through a man, the resurrection of the dead comes also through a man. For as in Adam all die, so in Christ (Al-Masih) all will be made alive.

But each in turn: Christ (Al-Masih), the firstfruits; then, when he comes, those who belong to him. Then the end will come, when he hands over the kingdom to God (Allah) the Father after he has destroyed all dominion, authority and power. For he must reign until he has put all his enemies under his feet. The last enemy to be destroyed is death.

1 CORINTHIANS 15:42-58

So will it be with the resurrection of the dead. The body that is sown is perishable, it is raised imperishable; it is sown in dishonor, it is raised in glory; it is sown in weakness, it is raised in power; it is sown a natural body, it is raised a spiritual body. If there is a natural body, there is also a spiritual body.

So it is written: "The first man Adam became a living being"; the last Adam, a life-giving spirit. The spiritual did not come first, but the natural, and after that the spiritual. The first man was of the dust of the earth; the second man is of heaven. As was the earthly man, so are those who are of the earth; and as is the heavenly man, so also are those who are of heaven. And just as we have borne the image of the earthly man, so shall we bear the image of the heavenly man.

I declare to you, brothers and sisters, that flesh and blood cannot inherit the kingdom of God (Allah), nor does the perishable inherit the imperishable. Listen, I tell you a mystery: We will not all sleep, but we will all be changed—in a flash, in the twinkling of an eye, at the last trumpet. For the trumpet will sound, the dead will be raised imperishable, and we will be changed. For the perishable must clothe itself with the imperishable, and the mortal with immortality.

When the perishable has been clothed with the imperishable, and the mortal with immortality, then the saying that is written will come true: "Death has been swallowed up in victory. Where, O death, is your victory? Where, O death, is your sting?"

The sting of death is sin, and the power of sin is the law. But thanks be to God (Allah)! He gives us the victory through our Lord Jesus Christ (Jesus Al-Masih). Therefore, my dear brothers and sisters, stand firm. Let nothing move you. Always give yourselves fully to the word of the Lord, because you know that your labor in the Lord is not in vain.

Please pause here and ponder what you've read.

- Explain the passages in your own words as if you were sharing it with someone else.
- Explain how the passages make you think or feel and why.
- What do the passages tell you about Allah?
- What do the passages tell you about you and your relationship with Allah?
- What action do you think Allah wants from you according to these passages?
- As a result, create an "I will . . ." statement to obey Allah according to these passages.

Scene in Heaven Just before Jesus Returns

Allah gives the prophet John a glimpse into heaven and the end times.

REVELATION 19:4-10

The twenty-four elders and the four living creatures fell down and worshiped God (Allah), who was seated on the throne. And they cried: "Amen, Hallelujah!"

Then a voice came from the throne, saying: "Praise our God, all you his servants, you who fear him, both great and small!" Then I heard what sounded like a great multitude, like the roar of rushing waters and like loud peals of thunder, shouting:

"Hallelujah! For our Lord God Almighty reigns. Let us rejoice and be glad and give him glory! For the wedding of the Lamb has come, and his bride has made herself ready. Fine linen, bright and clean, was given her to wear. (Fine linen stands for the righteous acts of God's holy people.)"

Then the angel said to me, "Write this: Blessed are those who are invited to the wedding supper of the Lamb!" And he added, "These are the true words of God (Allah)." At this I fell at his feet to worship him. But he said to me, "Don't do that! I am a fellow servant with you and with your brothers and sisters who hold to the testimony of Jesus. Worship God (Allah)! For it is the Spirit of prophecy who bears testimony to Jesus."

Return of the King

REVELATION 19:11-16

I saw heaven standing open and there before me was a white horse, whose rider is called Faithful and True. With justice he judges and wages war. His eyes are like blazing fire, and on his head are many crowns. He has a name written on him that no one knows but he himself. He is dressed in a robe dipped in blood, and his name is the Word of God (Allah). The armies of heaven were following him, riding on white horses and dressed in fine linen, white and clean.

Coming out of his mouth is a sharp sword with which to strike down the nations. "He will rule them with an iron scepter." He treads the winepress of the fury of the wrath of God Almighty (Allah Almighty). On his robe and on his thigh he has his name written: "KING OF KINGS AND LORD OF LORDS."

REVELATION 19:19-20

Then I saw the beast and the kings of the earth and their armies gathered together to wage war against the rider on the horse and his army. But the beast was captured, and with it the false prophet who had performed the signs on its behalf. With these signs he had deluded those who had received the mark of the beast and worshiped its image. The two of them were thrown alive into the fiery lake of burning sulfur.

The Thousand-Year Reign

REVELATION 20:1-6

And I saw an angel coming down out of heaven, having the key to the Abyss and holding in his hand a great chain. He seized the dragon, that ancient serpent, who is the devil, or Satan, and bound him for a thousand years. He threw him into the Abyss, and locked and sealed it over him, to keep him from deceiving the nations anymore until the thousand years were ended. After that, he must be set free for a short time.

I saw thrones on which were seated those who had been given authority to judge. And I saw the souls of those who had been beheaded because of their testimony about Jesus and because of the word of God (Allah). They had not worshiped the beast or its image and had not received its mark on their foreheads or their hands. They came to life and reigned with Christ (Al-Masih) a thousand years.

(The rest of the dead did not come to life until the thousand years were ended.) This is the first resurrection. Blessed and holy are those who share in the first resurrection. The second death has no power over them, but they will be priests of God (Allah) and of Christ (Al-Masih) and will reign with him for a thousand years.

Judgment Day for Satan

REVELATION 20:7-10

When the thousand years are over, Satan will be released from his prison and will go out to deceive the nations in the four corners of the earth—Gog and Magog—and to gather them for battle. In number they are like the sand on the seashore. They marched across the breadth of the earth and surrounded the camp of God's people, the city he loves. But fire came down from heaven and devoured them. And the devil, who deceived them, was thrown into the lake of burning sulfur, where the beast and the false prophet had been thrown. They will be tormented day and night for ever and ever.

Judgment Day for Humanity

REVELATION 20:11–15

Then I saw a great white throne and him who was seated on it. The earth and the heavens fled from his presence, and there was no place for them. And I saw the dead, great and small, standing before the throne, and books were opened. Another book was opened, which is the book of life. The dead were judged according to what they had done as recorded in the books.

The sea gave up the dead that were in it, and death and Hades gave up the dead that were in them, and each person was judged according to what they had done. Then death and Hades were thrown into the lake of fire. The lake of fire is the second death. Anyone whose name was not found written in the book of life was thrown into the lake of fire.

Please pause here and ponder what you've read.

- Explain the passages in your own words as if you were sharing it with someone else.
- Explain how the passages make you think or feel and why.
- What do the passages tell you about Allah?
- What do the passages tell you about you and your relationship with Allah?
- What action do you think Allah wants from you according to these passages?
- As a result, create an "I will . . ." statement to obey Allah according to these passages.

A New Heaven and a New Earth

REVELATION 21:1-4

Then I saw "a new heaven and a new earth," for the first heaven and the first earth had passed away, and there was no longer any sea. I saw the Holy City, the new Jerusalem, coming down out of heaven from God (Allah), prepared as a bride beautifully dressed for her husband.

And I heard a loud voice from the throne saying, "Look! God's (Allah's) dwelling place is now among the people, and he will dwell with them. They will be his people, and God (Allah) himself will be with them and be their God. He will wipe every tear from their eyes. There will be no more death or mourning or crying or pain, for the old order of things has passed away."

Allah Speaks from Heaven

REVELATION 21:5-8

He who was seated on the throne said, "I am making everything new!" Then he said, "Write this down, for these words are trustworthy and true."

He said to me: "It is done. I am the Alpha and the Omega, the Beginning and the End. To the thirsty I will give water without cost from the spring of the water of life. Those who are victorious will inherit all this, and I will be their God and they will be my children. But the cowardly, the unbelieving, the vile, the murderers, the sexually immoral, those who practice magic arts, the idolaters and all liars—they will be consigned to the fiery lake of burning sulfur. This is the second death."

The Bride

REVELATION 21:9-11

One of the seven angels who had the seven bowls full of the seven last plagues came and said to me, "Come, I will show you the bride, the wife of the Lamb." And he carried me away in the Spirit to a mountain great and high, and showed me the Holy City, Jerusalem, coming down out of heaven from God (Allah). It shone with the glory of God (Allah), and its brilliance was like that of a very precious jewel, like a jasper, clear as crystal.

REVELATION 21:22-27

I did not see a temple in the city, because the Lord God Almighty and the Lamb are its temple. The city does not need the sun or the moon to shine on it, for the glory of God (Allah) gives it light, and the Lamb is its lamp.

The nations will walk by its light, and the kings of the earth will bring their splendor into it. On no day will its gates ever be shut, for there will be no night there. The glory and honor of the nations will be brought into it. Nothing impure will ever enter it, nor will anyone who does what is shameful or deceitful, but only those whose names are written in the Lamb's book of life.

Paradise Restored

REVELATION 22:1-5

Then the angel showed me the river of the water of life, as clear as crystal, flowing from the throne of God (Allah) and of the Lamb down the middle of the great street of the city. On each side of the river stood the tree of life, bearing twelve crops of fruit, yielding its fruit every month. And the leaves of the tree are for the healing of the nations.

No longer will there be any curse. The throne of God (Allah) and of the Lamb will be in the city, and his servants will serve him. They will see his face, and his name will be on their foreheads. There will be no more night. They will not need the light of a lamp or the light of the sun, for the Lord God will give them light. And they will reign for ever and ever.

Jesus's Closing Statement

REVELATION 22:12-16

"Look, I am coming soon! My reward is with me, and I will give to each person according to what they have done. I am the Alpha and the Omega, the First and the Last, the Beginning and the End. Blessed are those who wash their robes, that they may have the right to the tree of life and may go through the gates into the city. Outside are the dogs, those who practice magic arts, the sexually immoral, the idolaters and everyone who loves and practices falsehood. I, Jesus, have sent my angel to give you this testimony for the churches. I am the Root and the Offspring of David, and the bright Morning Star."

Closing Statement of the Holy Spirit in the Holy Bible

REVELATION 22:17-21

The Spirit and the bride say, "Come!" And let the one who hears say, "Come!"' Let the one who is thirsty come; and let the one who wishes take the free gift of the water of life.

I warn everyone who hears the words of the prophecy of this scroll: If anyone adds anything to them, God (Allah) will add to that person the plagues described in this scroll. And if anyone takes words away from this scroll of prophecy, God (Allah) will take away from that person any share in the tree of life and in the Holy City, which are described in this scroll. He who testifies to these things says, "Yes, I am coming soon."

Amen. Come, Lord Jesus. The grace of the Lord Jesus be with God's people. Amen.

Please pause here and ponder what you've read.

- Explain the passages in your own words as if you were sharing it with someone else.
- Explain how the passages make you think or feel and why.
- What do the passages tell you about Allah?
- What do the passages tell you about you and your relationship with Allah?
- What action do you think Allah wants from you according to these passages?
- As a result, create an "I will . . ." statement to obey Allah according to these passages.

Sad Beginning for Humankind but a Hopeful Ending

As we move into the final section of this book, let's remember the tragic day humankind sinned and was removed from Paradise at the beginning of the Holy Bible and the blessed ending Allah offers.

GENESIS 3:22-24

And the Lord God said, "The man has now become like one of us, knowing good and evil. He must not be allowed to reach out his hand and take also from the tree of life and eat, and live forever."

So the Lord God banished him from the Garden of Eden to work the ground from which he had been taken. After he drove the man out, he placed on the east side of the Garden of Eden cherubim and a flaming sword flashing back and forth to guard the way to the tree of life.

Blessed Ending

REVELATION 22:1-2

... the river of the water of life ... flowing from the throne of God (Allah) and of the Lamb.... On each side of the river stood the tree of life ... And the leaves of the tree are for the healing of the nations.

REVELATION 21:3-4

... Look! God's (Allah's) dwelling place is now among the people, and he will dwell with them. They will be his people, and God (Allah) himself will be with them and be their God. He will wipe every tear from their eyes. There will be no more death or mourning or crying or pain, for the old order of things has passed away.

The Tree of Life is symbolic of Jesus Al-Masih. And only those whose names are found in the Book of Life are allowed to have this blessed ending of entering Paradise where the Tree of Life is. Let's look at what Allah reveals about the Book of Life.

The Book of Life

Here's what Allah reveals about the Book of Life before the Second Coming of Jesus Al-Masih:

REVELATION 3:5, JESUS AL-MASIH SAYS:

The one who is victorious will, like them, be dressed in white. I will never blot out the name of that person from the book of life, but will acknowledge that name before my Father and his angels.

REVELATION 13:8

All inhabitants of the earth will worship the beast—all whose names have not been written in the Lamb's book of life, the Lamb who was slain from the creation of the world.

In summary of Allah's revelations in the Holy Bible, He divides human beings into two categories:

1. Those who belong to the Lamb, Jesus Al-Masih, meaning those who accepted Jesus as Lord and Savior.
2. Those that willingly or ignorantly worshiped a false god or gods. If a human is believing in and worshipping any that is not the Triune (three in One) Allah of the Bible (Allah the Father, Allah the Son, Allah the Holy Spirit), then they are worshipping a false god or gods.

In Revelation 13:8, that false god is mysteriously referred to as the "beast." In Revelation, it is the "false prophet" that leads the world away from the One and only Allah to worship a false god.

Only those who accepted the Lamb as their Lord and Savior are in His Book of Life. Only they will be allowed to enter eternal Paradise with Allah.

Here's what Allah reveals about the Book of Life after the Second Coming of Jesus Al-Masih:

REVELATION 20:12
... Another book was opened, which is the book of life ...

REVELATION 20:15
Anyone whose name was not found written in the book of life was thrown into the lake of fire.

REVELATION 21:27
Nothing impure will ever enter it (Paradise) ... but only those whose names are written in the Lamb's book of life.

We have reviewed some of Allah's revelations about the Second Coming of Jesus Al-Masih, Judgment Day, and the return to Paradise of those who accepted Jesus as their Lord and Savior. Let us briefly review what Allah reveals about the followers of Jesus before the end times, here on earth—right now, in the past, and in the future until He returns.

Cost of Following Jesus

REVELATION 20:4
And I saw the souls of those who had been beheaded because of their testimony about Jesus and because of the word of God (Allah).

IN LUKE 14:27-33, JESUS SAYS THIS TO HIS POTENTIAL FOLLOWERS:
"And whoever does not carry their cross and follow me cannot be my disciple. Suppose one of you wants to build a tower. Won't you first sit down and estimate the cost to see if you have enough money to complete it? For if you lay the foundation and are not able to finish it, everyone who sees it will ridicule you, saying, 'This person began to build and wasn't able to finish.'

"So suppose a king is about to go to war against another king. Won't he first sit down and consider whether he is able with ten thousand men to oppose the one coming against him with twenty thousand? If he is not able, he will send a delegation while the other is still a long way off and will ask for terms of peace. In the same way, those of you who do not give up everything you have cannot be my disciples."

MATTHEW 10:16-22, JESUS SAYS THIS TO HIS DISCIPLES:

"I am sending you out like sheep among wolves. Therefore be as shrewd as snakes and as innocent as doves. Be on your guard; you will be handed over to the local councils and be flogged in the synagogues. On my account you will be brought before governors and kings as witnesses to them and to the Gentiles. But when they arrest you, do not worry about what to say or how to say it. At that time you will be given what to say, for it will not be you speaking, but the Spirit of your Father speaking through you.

"Brother will betray brother to death, and a father his child; children will rebel against their parents and have them put to death. You will be hated by everyone because of me, but the one who stands firm to the end will be saved."

MATTHEW 10:28-33, JESUS CONTINUES:

"Do not be afraid of those who kill the body but cannot kill the soul. Rather, be afraid of the One who can destroy both soul and body in hell. Are not two sparrows sold for a penny? Yet not one of them will fall to the ground outside your Father's care. And even the very hairs of your head are all numbered. So don't be afraid; you are worth more than many sparrows.

"Whoever acknowledges me before others, I will also acknowledge before my Father in heaven. But whoever disowns me before others, I will disown before my Father in heaven."

MATTHEW 10:38-39, JESUS CONTINUES:

"Whoever does not take up their cross and follow me is not worthy of me. Whoever finds their life will lose it, and whoever loses their life for my sake will find it."

MATTHEW 16:24-26 JESUS SAYS:

"... Whoever wants to be my disciple must deny themselves and take up their cross and follow me. For whoever wants to save their life will lose it, but whoever loses their life for me will find it. What good will it be for someone to gain the whole world, yet forfeit their soul? Or what can anyone give in exchange for their soul?"

Please pause here and ponder what you've read.

- Explain the passages in your own words as if you were sharing it with someone else.
- Explain how the passages make you think or feel and why.
- What do the passages tell you about Allah?
- What do the passages tell you about you and your relationship with Allah?
- What action do you think Allah wants from you according to these passages?
- As a result, create an "I will . . ." statement to obey Allah according to these passages.

Followers of Jesus may lose much, perhaps everything, even their life on earth, as a result of their obedience. In Luke 14, Jesus says that His followers must be willing to "give up everything." In

Matthew 10, Jesus encourages His followers to fear Allah more than they fear humans. In Matthew 16, Jesus reminds His followers to focus on eternal spiritual life rather than temporary physical life when facing persecution because of following Him.

Allah goes on throughout the rest of the Holy Bible to reveal that many of His followers will suffer and even experience horrible deaths. But Allah also reveals many promises about increasing eternal rewards for those who stand firm and endure to the end. The following are two passages of Holy Scriptures that are good examples of Allah's revealed promises.

Suffering and Eternal Rewards

1 PETER 1:3-9

Praise be to the God and Father of our Lord Jesus Christ (Jesus Al-Masih)! In his great mercy he has given us new birth into a living hope through the resurrection of Jesus Christ (Jesus Al-Masih) from the dead, and into an inheritance that can never perish, spoil or fade. This inheritance is kept in heaven for you, who through faith are shielded by God's (Allah's) power until the coming of the salvation that is ready to be revealed in the last time.

In all this you greatly rejoice, though now for a little while you may have had to suffer grief in all kinds of trials. These have come so that the proven genuineness of your faith—of greater worth than gold, which perishes even though refined by fire— may result in praise, glory and honor when Jesus Christ (Jesus Al-Masih) is revealed. Though you have not seen him, you love him; and even though you do not see him now, you believe in him and are filled with an inexpressible and glorious joy, for you are receiving the end result of your faith, the salvation of your souls.

2 CORINTHIANS 4:8-18

We are hard pressed on every side, but not crushed; perplexed, but not in despair; persecuted, but not abandoned; struck down, but not destroyed. We always carry around in our body the death of Jesus, so that the life of Jesus may also be revealed in our body. For we who are alive are always being given over to death for Jesus' sake, so that his life may also be revealed in our mortal body. So then, death is at work in us, but life is at work in you.

It is written: "I believed; therefore I have spoken." Since we have that same spirit of faith, we also believe and therefore speak, because we know that the one who raised the Lord Jesus from the dead will also raise us with Jesus and present us with you to himself. All this is for your benefit, so that the grace that is reaching more and more people may cause thanksgiving to overflow to the glory of God (Allah).

Therefore we do not lose heart. Though outwardly we are wasting away, yet inwardly we are being renewed day by day. For our light and momentary troubles are achieving for us an eternal glory that far outweighs them all. So we fix our eyes not on what is seen, but on what is unseen, since what is seen is temporary, but what is unseen is eternal.

Please pause here and ponder what you've read.

- Explain the passages in your own words as if you were sharing it with someone else.
- Explain how the passages make you think or feel and why.
- What do the passages tell you about Allah?
- What do the passages tell you about you and your relationship with Allah?

- What action do you think Allah wants from you according to these passages?
- As a result, create an "I will..." statement to obey Allah according to these passages.

Former Muslim Woman Endures Much

"Samra" came to America with her husband and children from a Middle Eastern Islamic country where sharing Jesus Al-Masih for the sake of conversion from Islam to Christianity is illegal.

Samra and her husband came to America to pursue business opportunities. Samra's husband was a very wealthy man. They lived in a large, very expensive house, in a very exclusive area. He provided Samra with a luxurious car, housemaids and assistants. The family had private teachers who taught their children at home. Samra's husband also gave her a large monthly allowance to spend as she pleased.

Sometime after they arrived in the United States, Samra was befriended by a Christian woman, "Paula." Paula shared with Samra her belief in Jesus Al-Masih as Lord and Savior. A devout and practicing Muslim, Samra quickly rejected that belief, and tried to convert Paula to Islam.

Eventually, Samra and Paula agreed to do an ongoing study together. Samra gave Paula an English translation of the Quran, while Paula gave Samra a Holy Bible. Then, they would get together at least once per week, sometimes twice, to study for an hour. They would spend thirty-minutes studying the Quran, then thirty minutes studying the Holy Bible. Samra later said that part of her strategy was to see what was in the Bible in order to find a way to persuade Paula into belief in Islam.

But after about eighteen months of regular study in the Bible, Samra believed in Jesus Al-Masih as her Lord and Savior. Upon learning about Samra's confession of faith in Al-Masih, her husband began abusing her. He beat her physically in an attempt to have Samra renounce her faith in Jesus and return to Islam. Samra did not.

So Samra's husband secretly bought airline tickets for him and the children to take them back to their country of origin. Samra, however, discovered the plan and took her own children into hiding with her new spiritual family—Christians who surrounded and supported her. Samra's husband eventually sold everything he owned in America, abandoned Samra and the children, and went back to his country of origin. Her own family of origin there disowned her as well.

Samra can never return with her children to their country of origin. If she ever did, she would have to renounce Christ and become a Muslim once again or face the death penalty.

After her confession of faith in Jesus, Samra literally went from prestige and wealth into financial poverty. She went from having maids and assistants to having to do everything on her own. She went from a luxurious home and car to a small place and an old car. She went from never having to work in her life outside the home to working hard to earn a meager living to support her and her children.

I asked Samra about her thought process leading up to the decision that turned her life upside down. Without hesitation, Samra turned to her Holy Bible and read two passages to me. First, Samra read Matthew 13:44–46 where Jesus Al-Masih says:

"The kingdom of heaven is like treasure hidden in a field. When a man found it, he hid it again, and then in his joy went and sold all he had and bought that field. Again, the kingdom of heaven is like a merchant looking for fine pearls. When he found one of great value, he went away and sold everything he had and bought it."

Then Samra read Mark 8:34–37 where Jesus Al-Masih says:

" . . . Whoever wants to be my disciple must deny themselves and take up their cross and follow me. For whoever wants to save their life will lose it, but whoever loses their life for me and for the gospel will save it. What good is it for someone to gain the whole world, yet forfeit their soul? Or what can anyone give in exchange for their soul?"

Samra told me that regardless of the earthly cost, she would do it over and over again. Samra said, "Jesus Al-Masih is worth it!"

How about you? Is Jesus Al-Masih worth that kind of potential earthly loss to you?

Former Muslim Man Is Killed

"Abdullah" is the oldest son of a very wealthy, influential, and politically powerful Muslim man in an Islamic country in the Middle East. The father was training up Abdullah to become his successor in everything.

When Abdullah was a boy, he heard on the radio a man say something about Jesus Al-Masih having been killed and resurrected, and that one day he would return from heaven to save those who believe in him. Very curious, he asked his father about it. His father told him that it was not true, and instructed Abdullah to ask the imam at the Masjid (Mosque in Arabic). Abdullah did. But the answers he heard from his father and the imam did not satisfy his curiosity.

Throughout the years, Abdullah asked other imams as well. The following is a summary of their responses as Abdullah described them to me: Christians believe that the Bible is Allah's word, so they believe what is in it. The Bible states that Jesus was killed and was raised from the dead. But the Bible, the imams said, was corrupted and Christians believe a lie.

Abdullah, however, had a very difficult time believing that human beings could somehow corrupt Allah's Holy Word. So eventually, he got a Holy Bible and read it. After about two years of studying it, Abdullah believed the Holy Bible was the true Word of Allah. Abdullah accepted Jesus Al-Masih as his Lord and Savior. Fearful of his father, Abdullah did not initially tell him about his new faith.

Abdullah studied the Holy Bible with one of his brothers, "Nader," who also believed in Jesus Al-Masih. Unlike Abdullah, Nader told his father about his new faith. For a while, Nader's father beat and tortured him so that he would deny his new faith in Jesus Al-Masih and believe Islam again. But Nader did not. The father discovered that Nader learned of Jesus Al-Masih from Abdullah.

The father brought Abdullah to where he had imprisoned Nader. With a gun, his father threatened to shoot him if he did not deny his faith in Jesus Al-Masih. Nader did not. So Abdullah's father shot and killed Nader right in front of him. The father then turned his aggression toward Abdullah, but he escaped successfully.

Abdullah escaped to a country that has religious freedom. Financially poor, Abdullah worked at whatever job he could get to survive. He spent his free time studying Allah's Word in the Holy Bible and shared the good news of Jesus Al-Masih with other Muslims who allowed him.

Meanwhile, Abdullah's father put a price on his son's life, instructing headhunters to find him and bring him home or kill him. While in the new country, Abdullah was found and beaten severely five times by such men. Seven other times, his father's men tried to kill him, but Abdullah survived and escaped each time.

One time, after Abdullah was stabbed with a knife by a man his father sent, I talked with him on the telephone while he was in the hospital. In severe pain, Abdullah told me that he felt like quitting sharing Jesus with Muslims anymore. Instead, he wanted to go into hiding in a new country where he could just live in peace. He was exhausted from the beatings and the attempts on his life. Abdullah asked me if I thought it acceptable that he just quit. I said yes.

A few months later, Abdullah called me to share with me the new decisions he made regarding whether he would share Jesus with Muslims. Abdullah decided that he is going to share Jesus with every Muslim he can. If someone beats him, then he will pray blessings upon them as they are beating him. If they stop, then as soon as he is healthy enough, then he will resume telling Muslims about Jesus. If they kill him, then he will be at peace with that, knowing that he will be escaping the sufferings of this life into eternal Paradise with Allah.

Sharing "The Good News"

Abdullah understood the commands of Jesus Al-Masih just before he returned to heaven after the Resurrection, and shared with me the following passages of Holy Scriptures:

MATTHEW 28:19–20

"Therefore go and make disciples of all nations, baptizing them in the name of the Father and of the Son and of the Holy Spirit, and teaching them to obey everything I have commanded you. And surely I am with you always, to the very end of the age."

ACTS 1:8

"But you will receive power when the Holy Spirit comes on you; and you will be my witnesses . . . to the ends of the earth."

Abdullah understood that this is what Allah expects from those who accept Jesus Al-Masih as Lord and Savior.

Suffering Because of Sharing

As we spoke on the phone, Abdullah turned to and read Philippians 1:12 from the Holy Bible, knowing the verse also applied to him. In the verse, Paul, a follower of Jesus, who was unjustly in jail because he was sharing the good news in Jesus Al-Masih said, *"Now I want you to know, brothers and sisters, that what has happened to me has actually served to advance the gospel."*

The "gospel" means the "good news." The gospel is the good news about what Allah did for us by sending Jesus Al-Masih as Ibn Allah from heaven to live a sinless life, die as Allah's required blood sacrifice on our behalf, overcome sin, death, and evil with the resurrection so that those who believe in and accept Jesus as Lord and Savior will be redeemed from hell into Paradise.

Let's continue reading the Holy Scriptures in Philippians 1:13–14 that was revealed while Paul was in prison:

As a result, it has become clear throughout the whole palace guard and to everyone else that I am in chains for Christ (Al-Masih). And because of my chains, most of the brothers and sisters have become confident in the Lord and dare all the more to proclaim the gospel without fear.

PHILIPPIANS 1:18–24

… The important thing is that in every way … Christ (Al-Masih) is preached. And because of this I rejoice. Yes, and I will continue to rejoice, for I know that through your prayers and God's (Allah's) provision of the Spirit of Jesus Christ (Jesus Al-Masih) what has happened to me will turn out for my deliverance. I eagerly expect and hope that I will in no way be ashamed, but will have sufficient courage so that now as always Christ (Al-Masih) will be exalted in my body, whether by life or by death.

For to me, to live is Christ (Al-Masih) and to die is gain. If I am to go on living in the body, this will mean fruitful labor for me. Yet what shall I choose? I do not know! I am torn between the two: I desire to depart and be with Christ (Al-Masih), which is better by far; but it is more necessary for you that I remain in the body.

Abdullah then turned to the Holy Scripture passage where it is revealed what Paul suffered in his life while sharing Al-Masih with those who did not know the gospel.

2 CORINTHIANS 11:24–28

Five times I received ... the forty lashes minus one. Three times I was beaten with rods, once I was pelted with stones, three times I was shipwrecked, I spent a night and a day in the open sea, I have been constantly on the move. I have been in danger from rivers, in danger from bandits, in danger from my fellow Jews, in danger from Gentiles; in danger in the city, in danger in the country, in danger at sea; and in danger from false believers.

I have labored and toiled and have often gone without sleep; I have known hunger and thirst and have often gone without food; I have been cold and naked. Besides everything else, I face daily the pressure of my concern for all the churches.

Allah's Message of Reconciliation

Abdullah then turned to 2 Corinthians chapter five, in which the Holy Spirit of Allah inspires the following through Paul as a command for all followers of Jesus Al-Masih.

2 CORINTHIANS 5:14–19

For Christ's (Al-Masih) love compels us, because we are convinced that one died for all, and therefore all died. And he died for all, that those who live should no longer live for themselves but for him who died for them and was raised again. So from now on we regard no one from a worldly point of view. Though we once regarded Christ (Al-Masih) in this way, we do so no longer.

Therefore, if anyone is in Christ (Al-Masih), the new creation has come: The old has gone, the new is here! All this is from God (Allah), who reconciled us to himself through Christ (Al-Masih) and gave us the ministry of reconciliation: that God (Allah) was reconciling the world to himself in Christ (Al-Masih), not counting people's sins against them. And he has committed to us the message of reconciliation.

Ambassadors for Jesus Al-Masih

2 CORINTHIANS 5:20-21

"We are therefore Christ's (Al-Masih's) ambassadors, as though God (Allah) were making his appeal through us. We implore you on Christ's (Al-Masih) behalf: Be reconciled to God (Allah). God (Allah) made him who had no sin to be sin for us, so that in him we might become the righteousness of God (Allah)."

Please pause here and ponder the verses that were shared in Abdullah and Samar's stories.

- Explain the passages in your own words as if you were sharing it with someone else.
- Explain how the passages make you think or feel and why.
- What do the passages tell you about Allah?
- What do the passages tell you about you and your relationship with Allah?
- What action do you think Allah wants from you according to these passages?
- As a result, create an "I will . . ." statement to obey Allah according to these passages.

The Rest of Abdullah's story

Since my encounter with Abdullah after he was stabbed, about five years before writing this book to you, he has faithfully obeyed Allah's commands for followers of Jesus Al-Masih. Abdullah has shared the gospel, the good news about Jesus Al-Masih, with thousands of Muslims. As of the writing of this book, more than 600 of these Muslims have believed in Jesus Al-Masih as Lord and Savior through Abdullah.

Chapter Sixteen

Allah's Expectations of YOU

There are no revelations from Allah in the Holy Bible where He expects believers in Jesus Al-Masih to quit their work and become full-time clergy. Nor are there any revelations where Allah expects you to lead a certain number of non-believers in Al-Masih to become believers.

Allah does, however, empower you, as Jesus Al-Masih promised in Acts 1:8: ". . . you will receive power when the Holy Spirit comes on you." And in Matthew 28:20 part b: "And surely I am with you always, to the very end of the age."

In summary of some of the Scriptures we have read, the Holy Spirit empowers you and me to share Allah's "message of reconciliation" and be "ambassadors" on behalf of Jesus Al-Masih, who is with you and me "to the very end of the age."

Allah expects us to share the gospel (the good news) whenever and wherever possible and appropriate. In words, works, in everything and in every way while living on earth, we represent Allah. Following are some of Allah's expectations of you and me:

1 CORINTHIANS 10:31
So whether you eat or drink or whatever you do, do it all for the glory of God (Allah).

COLOSSIANS 3:23-24
Whatever you do, work at it with all your heart, as working for the Lord, not for human masters, since you know that you will receive an inheritance from the Lord as a reward. It is the Lord Christ (Al-Masih) you are serving.

Allah Expects Disciples

Allah expects you and me to follow Jesus Al-Masih in words, works, and in everything and every way while living on earth. Allah expects you and me to become disciples of Jesus Al-Masih who help to make other disciples of Jesus Al-Masih. Let us conclude this final chapter of this book by studying some of Allah's revelations about that.

Let us review some details in the command Jesus gave just before He went back to heaven.

MATTHEW 28:19-20
"Therefore go and make disciples of all nations, baptizing them in the name of the Father and of the Son and of the Holy Spirit, and teaching them to obey everything I have commanded you. And surely I am with you always, to the very end of the age."

Jesus commanded His followers to go and make "disciples." By definition, a "disciple" is someone who follows the teachings of another. It is a follower or a learner. Applied to Jesus, a disciple is someone who learns from Him to live according to His ways and teachings in everything and in every way. In another summary of Allah's revelations in the Holy Bible, a disciple of Jesus Al-Masih is a worshiper, a faithful servant, and a witness.

A disciple of Jesus Al-Masih shares the gospel (the good news about Jesus) with others. A disciple helps others become disciples (faithful followers of Jesus) as well.

Let us review how to apply the above and other Scriptures to daily life right now by breaking it down into the next five steps for you.

1. Study Allah's revelations throughout the Holy Bible.

Continue on the journey of studying Allah's Word as we have done together since the beginning of this book. Here is a reminder passage about the Holy Bible from 2 Timothy 3:16–17:

All Scripture is God-breathed (Allah-breathed) and is useful for teaching, rebuking, correcting and training in righteousness, so that the servant of God (Allah) may be thoroughly equipped for every good work.

2. Obey Allah as you read and study His Word in the Holy Bible.

Continue the practice of pausing with Scriptures you learn and asking the six questions that were repeated throughout this book:

- Explain the passages in your own words as if you were sharing it with someone else.
- Explain how the passages make you feel and why.
- What do the passages tell you about Allah?

- What do the passages tell you about you and your relationship with Allah?
- What action do you think Allah wants from you according to these passages?
- As a result, create an "I will . . ." statement to obey Allah according to these passages.

This process is part of learning and doing what Allah revealed.

3. Get baptized.

In some countries, perhaps where you live, it may not be possible to be publicly baptized. Perhaps you do not know other followers of Jesus in your area. Or maybe public confession of faith in Jesus and baptism is life-threatening. If that is your case, then get baptized privately, just between you and Allah.

Otherwise, if possible, follow the example of Jesus Al-Masih and get baptized publicly. Here is that story just before Jesus Al-Masih began his earthly ministry as an adult.

MATTHEW 3:13–17

Then Jesus came from Galilee to the Jordan to be baptized by John (Yahya). But John tried to deter him, saying, "I need to be baptized by you, and do you come to me?"

Jesus replied, "Let it be so now; it is proper for us to do this to fulfill all righteousness."

Then John consented. As soon as Jesus was baptized, he went up out of the water. At that moment heaven was opened, and he saw the Spirit of God (Allah) descending like a dove and alighting on him. And a voice from heaven said, "This is my Son, whom I love; with him I am well pleased."

The following is a passage about new believers after hearing the gospel about Jesus from the Apostle Peter.

ACTS 2:37-38

When the people heard this, they were cut to the heart and said to Peter and the other apostles, "Brothers, what shall we do?"

Peter replied, "Repent and be baptized, every one of you, in the name of Jesus Christ (Jesus Al-Masih) for the forgiveness of your sins. And you will receive the gift of the Holy Spirit."

If possible, in your country where you live, seek Christian clergy for baptism in a church. In some countries, church buildings are not allowed. Church can be a group of Jesus's followers meeting together in a home to worship, pray, and study Allah's Word. That is the way it typically was during the first century after the resurrection of Jesus Al-Masih.

The symbolism of baptism includes but is not limited to the following:

- Baptism as modeled by Jesus is when a person is fully immersed in water.
- Baptism is a symbol of Jesus's burial and resurrection. Being immersed into the water and then coming up again during baptism identifies us with Jesus's death on the cross, His burial, and His resurrection from the dead.
- Public baptism is a public confession of your faith in, and commitment to, Jesus Al-Masih.
- Baptism is a symbol of your new life in Jesus Al-Masih. We bury the "old self," we are born again, rising from the water, to walk in a "new life" in Jesus, a new way of life that has to be followed through and lived out on a daily basis.
- Baptism is like a wedding ring; it is the outward symbol of the commitment you made in your heart.

4. Attend church regularly.

Again, church can be in a home or a building. It all depends on the situation in the country where you live. Here are a couple of Scriptures about Church, also referred to as the body of Jesus Al-Masih.

HEBREWS 10:24-25

And let us consider how we may spur one another on toward love and good deeds, not giving up meeting together, as some are in the habit of doing, but encouraging one another—and all the more as you see the Day approaching.

EPHESIANS 4:11-16

So Christ (Al-Masih) himself gave the apostles, the prophets, the evangelists, the pastors and teachers to equip his people for works of service, so that the body of Christ (Al-Masih) may be built up until we all reach unity in the faith and in the knowledge of the Son of God (Ibn Allah) and become mature, attaining to the whole measure of the fullness of Christ (Al-Masih).

Then we will no longer be infants, tossed back and forth by the waves, and blown here and there by every wind of teaching and by the cunning and craftiness of people in their deceitful scheming. Instead, speaking the truth in love, we will grow to become in every respect the mature body of him who is the head, that is, Christ (Al-Masih). From him the whole body, joined and held together by every supporting ligament, grows and builds itself up in love, as each part does its work.

5. Share the Gospel.

Allow the love of Jesus Al-Masih to compel you to tell others about Him, what you learned in the Holy Bible, how Allah is changing you, invite them to church, study Allah's Word with them, pray with them and for them.

MATTHEW 28:19
"Therefore go and make disciples."

ACTS 1:8
"You will be my witnesses."

2 CORINTHIANS 5:18-20
"All this is from God (Allah), who reconciled us to himself through Christ (Al-Masih) and gave us the ministry of reconciliation: that God (Allah) was reconciling the world to himself in Christ (Al-Masih), not counting people's sins against them. And he has committed to us the message of reconciliation. We are therefore Christ's (Al-Masih) ambassadors, as though God (Allah) were making his appeal through us."

In some countries, perhaps where you live, it may be illegal or dangerous to share the gospel with others. With that in mind, I am not telling you what to do specifically, especially since I do not know details of your situation. Please pray about how you can share the good news of Jesus with others, and let the Holy Spirit be your guide as to how to faithfully obey Allah in your specific circumstance.

Where There Are No Followers of Jesus

"Muhammad" is a retired politician in an Islamic country where there are no churches and it is illegal to share the gospel. Muhammad was a devout Muslim and raised his four sons and three daughters to be the same. The father of his wife is one of the top imams in the country.

As a young man, when Muhammad was a soldier in the military, he was involved in a military conflict between Islamic extremists and American military soldiers. While retrieving the body of an American soldier killed during a fierce battle between the two sides, Muhammad found a Holy Bible. Curious about the contents of the Holy Bible, Muhammad secretly kept it and brought it home with him.

Initially, Muhammad did not read the Holy Bible. He hid it away. Busy with his career, family, and life in general, he didn't think much about it. But as he neared retirement, Muhammad began reading the Holy Bible he had hidden for so long. After about three years of studying, Muhammad secretly became a believer in Jesus Al-Masih as his Lord and Savior. Muhammad did not share his new faith with anyone else. He was fearful that any of the devout Muslims he knew, including his own sons, might kill him if they found out.

One day while at the souk (marketplace), Muhammad met an American, "Gary." A friendship was born between the two and grew to the point where they trusted each other enough to share secrets with one another. Muhammad confided to Gary that he was a secret follower of Jesus. Gary confided to Muhammad that he was in the area seeking to start a secret house church so that Muslims there could hear the gospel, and become disciples, witnesses, and ambassadors for Jesus Al-Masih.

Gary returned to America without starting a church in the area, and Muhammad is still the only believer in Jesus Al-Masih in that area that they are aware of. But Muhammad and Gary talk regularly on the telephone and online, studying Allah's Word and praying together. Gary is preparing to return to that area to start a house church.

As of the writing of this book, it is still not clear for Muhammad when and how he is to share his faith in Jesus Al-Masih with family and friends. He did ask Gary for guidance regarding the situation.

Gary responded to Muhammad as I would respond: "Please continue to study and grow in the Word of Allah in the Holy Bible. Continue to pray that the Holy Spirit will make your next steps clear and that He will give you the faith to follow the path in obedience."

Pray about your specific path as a new follower of Jesus Al-Masih. Allah is not surprised by your situation in your area, or with your family and friends.

- If you have a Christian friend, then ask him or her to pray with you.
- If you do not know or have access to a Christian near you, then please contact us with your specific prayer request (pray@WordofAllah.org).

Remember!

EPHESIANS 2:4–10

. . . because of his great love for us, God (Allah), who is rich in mercy, made us alive with Christ (Al-Masih) even when we were dead in transgressions—it is by grace you have been saved. And God (Allah) raised us up with Christ (Al-Masih) and seated us with him in the heavenly realms in Christ Jesus, in order that in the coming ages he might show the incomparable riches of his grace, expressed in his kindness to us in Christ Jesus.

For it is by grace you have been saved, through faith—and this is not from yourselves, it is the gift of God (Allah)—not by works, so that no one can boast. For we are God's (Allah's) handiwork created in Christ Jesus to do good works, which God (Allah) prepared in advance for us to do.

The Armor of Allah

EPHESIANS 6:10-20

Finally, be strong in the Lord and in his mighty power. Put on the full armor of God (Allah), so that you can take your stand against the devil's schemes. For our struggle is not against flesh and blood, but against the rulers, against the authorities, against the powers of this dark world and against the spiritual forces of evil in the heavenly realms.

Therefore, put on the full armor of God (Allah), so that when the day of evil comes, you may be able to stand your ground, and after you have done everything, to stand. Stand firm then, with the belt of truth buckled around your waist, with the breastplate of righteousness in place, and with your feet fitted with the readiness that comes from the gospel of peace. In addition to all this, take up the shield of faith, with which you can extinguish all the flaming arrows of the evil one.

Take the helmet of salvation and the sword of the Spirit, which is the word of God (Allah). And pray in the Spirit on all occasions with all kinds of prayers and requests. With this in mind, be alert and always keep on praying for all the Lord's people. Pray also for me, that whenever I speak, words may be given me so that I will fearlessly make known the mystery of the gospel, for which I am an ambassador in chains. Pray that I may declare it fearlessly, as I should.

About the Author

After enduring intense persecution as a Christian raised in Islamic countries, anger toward Muslims filled Renod Bejjani's heart, and he stopped believing in Allah. For twenty years, he searched for meaning. He looked for answers in science and explored the world's major religions. Through all he read and studied, including the Quran and the Holy Bible, Bejjani became a believer in Allah because of His Word in the Holy Bible.

Allah removed the anger and hate from Bejjani's bitter heart and replaced it with His healing, peace, and love for everyone—including Muslims. Since 2011, Bejjani and his wife, Karen, have shared the love of Allah with thousands of Muslims worldwide. They founded iHOPE Ministries to help other Christians experience the same transformation, and Allah has blessed the ministry with thousands of Christian students worldwide who now also love Muslims and share the love of Allah with them.

www.ingramcontent.com/pod-product-compliance
Lightning Source LLC
Chambersburg PA
CBHW050313120526
44592CB00014B/1885